Outrageous

One Act Plays
by
Miguel Piñero

Arte Público Press
Houston

Acknowledgements

Special thanks to Joseph Papp and the New York Shakespeare Festival, Bill Bushnell and the Los Angeles Actors Theatre, Nicolás Kanellos, Miguel Algarín, Rosa from 8th Street, Johnny Boy, Rick Van Valkenburg, Jimmy Baca, and my heart Mala.

Photographs of Miguel Piñero by Arlene Gottfried.

This volume is made possible by a grant from the National Endowment for the Arts, a federal agency.

This book was purchased by the Allen County Public Library Foundation with funds donated by library supporters to match a National Endowment for the Humanities challenge grant for the purchase of books in the humanities fields.

Arte Público Press
University of Houston
University Park
Houston, Texas 77004

OUTRAGEOUS

Table of Contents

For my son Pito

Just remember this, my son:
Sometime you feel the light
and do not see the sun.
In between a rock and a hard place
there lies truth.
You are the one
you have always been looking for.

For my godson Antonio

Tend your heart to the past,
never rush to go too fast,
'cause when you're cool for twenty,
you get paid for twenty-one.

God bless,
Miguel

Introduction

I first met Miguel Pinero in 1972,
shortly after his release from Sing Sing
penitentiary, where for the past year he had
found the courage to write and develop a play
called SHORT EYES about the very place in
which he was living. The following year I
produced that play, which proved to be one of
the most powerful dramas ever seen at New
York's Public Theater, and later moved it to
Lincoln Center for a highly successful run.
If the unnerving honesty of SHORT EYES, as
well as the raw corrosive force of its
language, sometimes appeared to be too much
for middle class audiences, the work
nevertheless won the New York Drama Critics'
Award for best play of the season. With this
first and best known of his many plays,
Miguel has probably had more impact on
younger writers than any Latin playwright of
his generation.
From Francois Villon to Jean Genet,
Miguel belongs to a tradition of writers
whose devious and renegade lives paradoxi-
cally result in the most painstaking devotion
to the truth and rigor of their craft. All
dramatists of real value must sooner or later
confront what for them is truly dangerous,
either within themselves or in the outside
world. That we the audience feel that danger
and understand something of what it is about
is often what makes a play important and
durable. If the life of Miguel seems illusive
and troubling, one can only applaud what is
so candidly engaged here by his art, where
very little is stolen or borrowed and a great
deal is revealed. In this sense Miguel
Pinero is as blessed and as straight a writer
as they come.

Joseph Papp

Paper Toilet

Paper Toilet

Paper Toilet is a one-act play that takes place in a subway toilet. The rumble of trains is heard.

The People in the Play:

MAN 1:   *Middle aged.*
MAN 2:   *Early twenties.*
MAN 3:   *Middle aged vice cop.*
MAN 4:   *Late twenties.*
BOY 1:   *15 years old.*
BOY 2:   *14 years old.*
WOMAN: *Middle aged.*
COP 1:   *Early thirties.*
COP 2:   *Early thirties*

A man rushes into the toilet. He is excited, stops in front of the pay toilet stall, searches his pockets . . . mumbles some curses, begins to get more and more jittery with each rumble a through different pocket. Cursing, he finally crawls under the toilet stall door. A loud satisfying grunt is heard.

MAN 1:   Goddamn it, things are so up tight nowadays, you gotta pay to take a lousy shit . . .

MAN 2:   *(Entering.)* Now to work . . . *(Takes a position in front of one of the urinals.)*

Another man enters and takes a place next to Man 2. A few seconds later another man comes in and does likewise.

MAN 4:   *(To nobody.)* My . . . my . . . the tearoom is crowded early today.

MAN 2:   Did you say something to me?

MAN 4:   No nothing at all . . . I talk to myself when I pee.

MAN 2:   Good enough . . .

MAN 4:   What is good enough, the size or the thickness or the color?

MAN 2:   What are you talking about?

MAN 4:   Good enough.

MAN 2:   What is good enough?

MAN 4:   Really.

MAN 2:   Really what?

MAN 4:   Who knows, perhaps the flavor of it . . . some people taste like wet rubber . . . don't you agree?

MAN 2:   I really don't know what you're talking about.

MAN 4:   You don't?

MAN 2:   No I don't . . . and I like my peeing to be private.

MAN 4:   Then you should do it at home behind the locked door of your bathroom and not in a subway toilet.

10

MAN 3:   Well, when you got to go you got to go.

MAN 2:   That's the way nature intended it to be like, I believe . . .

MAN 4:   So do I.

MAN 2:   So do you what?

MAN 4:   Believe it to be like . . .

MAN 2:   Yes, well if you don't mind, I'd like to cut this conversation short, you see?

MAN 4:   I see very well. What do you want me to look at?

MAN 2:   You see, I can't pee and talk at the same time.

MAN 4:   You don't have the coordination to do so?

MAN 2:   No, I don't . . . so if you please, get to your own peeing business and leave me to mine.

MAN 3:   You know, I am the same way, I can't piss if someone is watching me or if I believe someone is watching me or talking to me. I guess it has to do with something from early childhood.

MAN 4:   You should go see a therapist.

MAN 3:   They have peeing therapists?

MAN 4:   They have all kinds of therapists, it's big business nowadays to specialize in some kind of therapy.

MAN 2:   Really?

MAN 4:   Yes, no kidding around. I once heard of a therapist who specialized in nose picking.

MAN 2:   Jesus H. Fucking Christ, will you shut up and let me pee?!!

MAN 4:   I didn't know I was holding you back.

Silence. Pause. MAN 4 takes a look at MAN 3's penis. MAN 3 catches him. MAN 4 smiles and looks at the ceiling. MAN 4 takes another long look at MAN 3's penis again. This time he turns his head away before being detected. Once more he takes another look at MAN 3's penis. MAN 2 catches him.

MAN 2:   Hey, whacha gonna do, suck out his dick with
           your eyes?
MAN 4:   Who me?
MAN 2:   Yeah, you, who else is here standing gawking at
           his dick? I'm talking to you mister . . . don't act
           funny with me. I know your type. You come into
           these places waiting for school boys to come in,
           and stare at them . . . you ain't gonna deny it are
           you? Well, where are you going? Go on, run. Go
           on, run, fairy . . . all alike . . . sick . . . freaking
           faggots . . . they come into these places to play
           hide and seek with other people's cocks . . . gotta
           watch them.
MAN 3:   The cocks?
MAN 2:   No, them freaks. You know what I mean.
MAN 3:   No, I don't know.
MAN 2:   Take it from me, I know. I been coming to these
           places long enough to know what I'm talking
           about.
MAN 3:   I guess so.
MAN 2:   Well, I know so.
MAN 3:   I guess you do.
MAN 2:   What you reading, the sports? Who won last
           night's game between . . .
MAN 3:   I am not reading anything at all . . . I'm trying
           to take a piss in peace . . . if you want to read the
           paper while you pee, here, read it.
MAN 2:   Shove it.
MAN 1:   I would like to read it.

*MAN 3 begins to exit. MAN 2 simulates masturbation. MAN 3
enters again.*

MAN 3:   Well . . . well . . . my . . . my . . . you have a
           big one for a white man. Can I clean it for

12

you . . . here I have some kleenex tissues. They're supposed to be good for everything . . . even life juice. Here, let me help you up . . . ah, don't be shy . . . don't be embarassed. Everybody should jerkoff now and then . . . it's good for the spirit and not to mention the wrist . . . you know what I mean?

MAN 2:   No, thanks, I got a handkerchief, thank you.

MAN 3:   No need to reward me, put your wallet back in your pocket. Just let me hold it for a while, that'll be reward enough for me.

MAN 2:   Shut up.

MAN 3:   No need to shout . . . oh, the man in the stall . . . well, don't worry about him, he's probably looking to do the same thing, just like little ole me . . . now ain't that something?

MAN 2:   Shut up and look at this. Does this look like money to you?

MAN 3:   No, it looks like a badge.

MAN 2:   That's just what it is . . . you are under arrest . . . soliciting for the purpose of an unnatural sex act.

MAN 3:   This has to be an act.

MAN 2:   No, it's very real my friend.

MAN 3:   If it's for real, I ain't no friend of yours (Goes into fit of cursing.)

MAN 2:   Oh, shut the fuck up, already will you? Ain't you ever been locked up before. Every nigger in New York has been in jail and that's the way God meant it to be. Wow, it stinks in here. Hey, you in there, you in that combat zone, why don't you flush that stink out to the river before it hits the streets and I have to come back and summons you for polluting the air.

MAN 3:   Ha, ha . . . very funny, you're a real comedian ala Bob Hope . . .

MAN 2: The air is gonna get so bad I'm gonna have to call Ralph Nader on you . . . ha . . . ha . . .

MAN 3: Jesus Christ . . .

MAN 1: Did you call my name out in vain?

MAN 3: Everybody's a comedian on the day I get arrested, shit!

MAN 1: That's what I'm doing.

MAN 2: Do it in good health.

MAN 1: Well, some come to sit and think . . . I came here to shit and stink.

MAN 2: You sure accomplished what you set out to do, mister. Okay, come on, let's go, come on, on the double.

MAN 3: What, I'm back in the army now.

MAN 1: Holy shit, no fucking toilet paper! You pay to get in here and they don't have the decency to protect you from the toilet paper thieves . . . shit . . . shit . . . shit . . . the newspaper . . . saved by the daily.

A young boy enters fast talking with another who is excited.

BOY 1: Boy, I bet there's a thousand dollars in that purse.

BOY 2: The way she fought for it and screamed and carried on, there must be a whole lot more than that. Man I bet there's a million . . .

BOY 1: I'd settle for twenty dollars.

BOY 2: Me too.

BOY 1: Let's check the motherfucker out, man. Open up the damn thing.

BOY 2: Okay, don't rush . . . man, don't rush man, be cool . . . be cool.

BOY 1: Be cool, are you kidding me? Shit, that bitch just gave us the fight of the century for this shit here and you tell me to be cool. Man, you better be

14

cool and open up that damn thing, brother.

BOY 2:   I dragged that old bitch down them stairs kicking.

BOY 1:   She screamed like a fucking police siren. What a mouth.

BOY 2:   Man, I almost had to stomp that bitch's back string loose before she cut loose of that damn bag.

BOY 1:   Let's see what we got, brotherman.

BOY 2:   Kicked her head in . . .

BOY 1:   The regular junk . . .

BOY 2:   Wrestled all over the platform, almost fell into the tracks.

BOY 1:   Welfare card.

BOY 2:   Should have let her fall . . . let the train deal with her.

BOY 1:   Nothing in the little wallet . . .

BOY 2:   Boy, lucky for us that the fucking strap broke or we'd be still struggling with that old big black mother jumbo.

BOY 1:   My father always says, son, with people's wives . . . brothers . . . sisters . . . fuck over their whole generation . . . but don't fuck with their money.

BOY 2:   My mom says, don't fuck with a wino's bottle or a junkie's cooker.

BOY 1:   My father always says, son, take this advice, it's the only one that I can give freely, with confidence and experience, then he shows me a pack of scars all over his body . . . cuz if you take this advice, boy,about not fucking with other peoples money, especially when they need it badder than you, you best be cool, and you'll live to see my age. Then he takes a toke and passes out and that bottle be as empty as his advice.

BOY 2:   Later for your pop, man. I can't seem to find any bread in this purse, man.

BOY 1:   The hag has to have something in the bag. Like nobody fights like that for nothing, man.

BOY 2:   Nothing, man, not a fucking thing, shitfuckbitchfaggot-motherfuck!

BOY 1:   Man, the way that bitch fought for the fucking purse, I thought we had hit Rockerfella's grandmother, man.

BOY 2:   It's your fault . . .

BOY 1:   My fault?

BOY 2:   59 cents . . . 59 cents. Ain't this a kick in the motherfucking ass?

BOY 1:   My fault, what you talking, nigger? You crazy shit, how the fuck can this be my fault, motherfucker?

BOY 2:   You said that she was a bet, man. You said she a bet.

BOY 1:   Man, the way she were holding on to that damn thing, man, what else am I to think, shit, man, be cool . . . man, she had to have something in there.

BOY 2:   Maybe in the lining of the purse.

BOY 1:   Yeah, rip it open brother . . .

BOY 2:   Motherrrrffffuuuckkkerrrrr!

BOY 1:   Damn, no way, man, she had to have something there . . . the bitch held on to it too tight, man, to be nothing . . . maybe a welfare check.

BOY 2:   There ain't nothing in there . . . what if we had gotten busted for that . . . man, that's getting busted for nothing.

BOY 1:   Man, I didn't force you to go with me . . . I ain't got no gun.

BOY 2:   Man, this is the last time I ever listen to you on anything again . . . the motherfucking last time, brother.

BOY 1:   Man, fuck you.

BOY 2:   Fuck you too, shit . . . you ain't nothing man.

BOY 1:   Man, fuck you, and if you don't like it, jump, faggot.

BOY 2:   Motherfucker, put your hands down before I put your jaw down.

BOY 1:   Man, throw what you got, punk, and throw your best shit, 'cause you ain't saying a pound, punk . . .

BOY 2:   Man, what you gonna do, you gonna fight me with your hands or with your mouth?

BOY 1:   If you move your hands, I'm gonna move your teeth . . .

BOY 2:   You got more shit with you than this fucking toilet.

MAN 1:   Boys . . .

BOY 1:   Who the fuck you calling "boy"?

BOY 2:   Man, you better dig yourself, faggot.

MAN 1:   I don't mean it in any manner that's derogatory, gentlemen.

BOY 1:   What the hell you talking about, nigger?

BOY 2:   Speak up when a man talks to you, sucker.

MAN 1:   Excuse me, please, I meant no harm. I apologize, I really mean it. Believe me, I meant no harm whatsoever . . . I was only trying to capture your attention.

BOY 1:   What you say?

BOY 2:   Say he wanna rap.

MAN 1:   I couldn't help overhearing about your little, let's say, financial adventure and about the frustrating results. I'd like to engage you in a little business.

BOY 1:   Man, what the fuck you talking about, sucker?

BOY 2:   He say he peeped into our comb, man.

BOY 1:   Man, you better learn to mind your own business, you could get all hurt up doing shit like that.

MAN 1:   I didn't mean to pry, just that your failure . . .

BOY 2:	Man, my father is a failure, but not me, mother-fucker. I ain't no failure.
BOY 1:	Not yet, anyway.
MAN 1:	I have a proposition to make . . .
BOY 1:	He got a what to make?
BOY 2:	I think the dude wanna play the skin flute, man.
BOY 1:	Say man, are you a faggot or something?
MAN 1:	I might be a motherfucker, but I'm not a faggot, young man?
BOY 1:	What the deal, man?
BOY 2:	We ain't icing nobody for nobody.
MAN 1:	What was that?
BOY 1:	What the deal?
MAN 1:	Oh, the deal, yes, the deal, the deal is nothing that will get any of you in any kind of trouble. What I would like is . . . I would like to obtain that newspaper that I left on the floor over there. I . . . I . . . was reading an important article.
BOY 1:	Cut the shit, you want the paper, huh? Why don't you come out and get it yourself?
MAN 1:	Obviously because . . .
BOY 1:	Man, you ain't got no shit paper and you wanna cop the news to do the job, right?
BOY 2:	But we ain't upping the motherfucker unless you is upping something for it.
MAN 1:	I was planning to offer a reward.
BOY 1:	Like what, motherfucker?
BOY 2:	Better be good . . .
MAN 1:	Well, it is my newspaper. I left it behind.
BOY 2:	Now you wanna use it for the behind.
MAN 1:	I said that I would buy it from you at a very reasonable price.
BOY 1:	Like what?
MAN 1:	One dollar.
BOY 1:	One dollar, are you serious, man?

BOY 2:	Naw, man he just joking, ain't you mister?
MAN 1:	Apiece . . . one dollar apiece.
BOY 1:	That hold my interest a little bit.
BOY 2:	. . . Cuz you know the old saying, "finders keepers, losers weepers."
BOY 1:	That old saying and, besides, we were planning to read the paper, anyway.
BOY 2:	That's right, so like we couldn't cut it loose for nothing.
MAN 1:	I understand and I apologize for making such a meager offer for such a valuable piece of merchandise. It was unthinkable.
BOY 1:	So, why you say it then?
MAN 1:	So, in that light, I will offer each of you two dollars . . . consider it a reward.
BOY 1:	*(Whispers.)* I think that dude has some bucks.
BOY 2:	*(Whispers.)* I do too.
BOY 1:	Two dollars for a newspaper, that unreal . . .
MAN 1:	Well, do we have a deal?
BOY 1:	Hey, man, you got any more money on you?
BOY 2:	Well, man, answer up, mister.
MAN 1:	I don't have any real money on me.
BOY 1:	What you got, counterfeit, motherfucker?

They grab the man's pants and begin a tug of war with them. They are cursing and threatening to end up with his pants.

BOY 1:	And, motherfucker, you better stay in that fucking toilet.
BOY 2:	Goddamn, we hit the number, fifty motherfucking dollars, bro.
MAN 1:	Please, let me have my pants back.
BOY 1:	Boy, you beg a lot, don't you, motherfucker?
BOY 2:	He sure do, you a begging fool . . .
MAN 1:	Please, keep the money . . . just give me back my pants.

BOY 1:   You want the newspaper too?
MAN 1:   Yes.
BOY 2:   Then, be cool.

A big, rugged looking woman enters.

WOMAN: I thought I'd find you creeps in one of these places counting my money.
BOY 1:   Counting your what, bitch?
BOY 2:   Money? What motherfucking money you talking about, 59 cents? Is that what you call money?
WOMAN: Where's my money?
BOY 1:   Here . . . here, lady, here's your freaking bag. Now get the fuck out of here before we rip you off again.
BOY 2:   Rip her off again, for what? The bitch ain't got shit.
WOMAN: Rape . . . me . . . rape me, really? . . .
MAN 1:   Lady, would you ask them to give me my pants.
BOY 1:   Shut up in there, faggot.
BOY 2:   You heard the man, don't make us repeat ourselves, motherfucker.
BOY 1:   Get that clear, now mister. We ain't playing no games.
WOMAN: And neither am I. Now I want my money.
BOY 1:   Lady, there ain't no money to give you, cuz you had no money to take in the first place.
WOMAN: First you take my money. Now you tell me that there wasn't none. Then you say you gonna rape me off again.
BOY 1:   Rape, who said anything about rape? Shit, you must be crazy, bitch. To think anyone would wanna fuck you. Shit, bitch, you look so bad, I wouldn't fuck you with his dick. Shit, lady, you so old, I'd end up with lock jaw on my wood.

BOY 2:   Purple balls . . . imagine her on the bed naked. You's a sorry sight, lady. Shit, you spoil a wet dream.

BOY 1:   And you stink bad, too.

WOMAN: If you don't give me my money I'll scream and tell the cops that you armed robbery me and tried to rape me, too.

MAN 1:   I'll be your witness, lady.

WOMAN: Man, shut the fuck up and flush that damn thing out of here.

BOY 1:   Man, if you don't shut up, you'll be reading about yourself in the motherfucking newspaper you wanted so bad.

BOY 2:   "Man drowns in subway toilet bowel."

WOMAN: Now give me my money, fellas, cuz once I start hollering, even God gonna come down and check it out too.

BOY 1:   Tell him Satan is waiting for him.

BOY 2:   And he ready to deal.

WOMAN: Fuck God, deal with me, you little bunch of faggots.

BOY 1:   And, lady, you can scream rape all the fuck you want, cuz no one in their right mind, cop or judge, would ever believe we try to rape something as ugly as you, not even if you swear to that on a stack of bibles ten feet high.

She sails into them screaming, fist flying, cursing. They slap her upside the head with the newspaper and hit her with the pants. She throws one on the floor.

COP 1:   Okay, hold it . . . what the hell is going on in here?

WOMAN: They armed robbery me and they tried to rape me, officer.

21

COP 1:   They tried to do what?
BOY 1:   You don't believe that?!
BOY 2:   She try to kill us.
COP 1:   That I believe . . .
COP 2:   What the hell are you doing in the men's toilet, lady? Is this part of the women's liberation movement or something?
WOMAN: It's nothing. They robbery me and try to rape me. Help me arrest them. I demand that you arrest them now.
COP 1:   Be quiet, lady, will you please?

A row of accusations begins between the boys and the woman.

MAN 1:   Would anyone care to give me my pants or the newspaper, please?
COP 1:   Hey you in there, shut up or we'll run you in for obstructing justice . . . you hear me, Mack? . . . and flush that damn thing.
MAN 1:   But officer, I need that newspaper.
ALL: SHUT UP!

More accusations and arguments.

COP 2:   Hold it, lady, hold it, lady!
COP 1:   You two guys, shut the fuck up right now.
BOY 1:   But officer . . .
COP 1:   Not another fucking word, you hear me?
BOY 1:   Yes, sir.
BOY 2:   Be cool, bro, be cool.
WOMAN: They trying to be cool, so they can escape into the tracks.
BOY 1:   She crazy.
COP 1:   What did you say?
BOY 1:   I didn't say anything, officer.

BOY 2:   Be cool, man, be cool.

COP 1:   Listen to your friend, be cool.

WOMAN: They beat me and robbed me.

COP 1:   Lady, please be quiet. We'll get to the bottom of this as soon as we get some cooperation.

COP 2:   Okay, now, what the hell you doing in the men's toilet?

WOMAN: I was robbery by them there two boys. They beat me, they try to rape me.

COP 2:   Lady . . . lady, hold it. We're here to get the facts, not fantasies. Please stick to what really happened.

WOMAN: That's what really happened. They try to rape me . . .

BOY 2:   The only thing we raped was your pocket book.

BOY 1:   Now, who not being cool!

COP 1:   So, you snatched her purse, huh?

BOY 2:   Man, I didn't say that, you did.

COP 2:   How would you like a size 9 up up your ass, kid?

COP 1:   Lady, if they try to rape you, they don't belong in a prison, but in a mental health institution.

WOMAN: They robbed me and beat me up.

BOY 1:   That's a lot of shit. You were doing all the beating up.

BOY 2:   Man, she almost killed us.

COP 1:   Maybe we arrived too early, huh?

COP 2:   Maybe we did.

COP 1:   You think if we step outside for a while, they'll finish each other up?

COP 2:   I don't know, but I feel that this is going to be one of them nights.

COP 1:   Any of you got a knife?

BOY 1:   We don't carry weapons of any kind.

COP 1:   Yeah, I bet both of you sing in the choir on Sundays.

23

BOY 2:   As a matter of fact, we do.

COP 1:   Jesus.

BOY 1:   He saves.

COP 1:   Oh, shut up, will ya?

COP 2:   Kid, we're trying to be nice guys. Why not just take our word for it that if you keep opening your trap, we're not going to be nice guys and you're gonna start screaming police brutality. So keep your fucking mouth shut.

BOY 1:   Yes, sir.

COP 1:   Do you understand?

BOY 1:   Yes, sir.

BOY 2:   Yes, sir.

COP 1:   Good, now back to you, miss. Why are you in the men's toilet?

WOMAN: Because this is where they ran to escape from me.

MAN 1:   Can I say something?

COP 1:   Later . . . right now, keep pushing and keep your mouth shut.

MAN 1:   I'm going to write my congressman about this.

COP 1:   Write to the fucking mayor, mister.

COP 2:   You wanna pen? Here, use the fucking toilet paper.

MAN 1:   There isn't any toilet paper. That's what I'm trying to tell you.

COP 1:   Well, I guess that's your tough luck, isn't it?

COP 2:   Now, keep out of this investigation.

WOMAN: Now, what I was saying is that these two birds here . . .

COP 2:   Watch your language, lady, please.

WOMAN: You're New York City cops and you're telling me to watch my language?!

COP 1:   Lady, don't give us a hard time, please.

24

Enter vice cop.

VICE COP: What's this, what's all this about?
COP 1:   Who are you?
VICE COP: Police Vice Squad.
COP 1:   Got some identification, sir?
VICE: Here, what's that, a play thing?
COP 1:   Sorry, sir.
VICE COP: Now, what's all this about?
COP 1:   That's what we're trying to figure out.
WOMAN: And they ain't doing it, telling everybody to shut up all the time, not giving anyone a chance to say anything at all. These two are not what I call cops.
COP 1:   No, lady? What do you call a cop?
WOMAN: A flatfoot.
COP 1:   Jesus, lady, get with the times. They now call us pigs.
COP 2:   Pride, integrity, guts.
BOY 1:   That's a lot of bullshit.
VICE COP: Who are they?
COP 1:   We're trying to find out who's making a complaint. They for assault. Her, for armed robbery and attempted rape.
VICE COP: Rape. Ahahahahah. You're kidding.
COP 1:   I wish we were. She insists that they tried it.
COP 2:   Do you believe it?
VICE COP: They must be crazy or awful horny.
COP 1:   Okay, once again, what did they hit you with?
WOMAN: With the newspaper.
COP 1:   Assault with a dangerous instrument.
COP 2:   Got it.
WOMAN: They also try to strangle me with them pants over there.
COP 1:   Attempted murder. Take the pants too.

COP 2:   Got it.

COP 1:   Okay, lady, come on to the precinct and sign a complaint. On second thought, why not just meet us there.

BOY 1:   Look, man, we snatched the book, but we didn't try no rape, man.

COP 1:   Don't worry about it.

VICE COP: Wait a second, not so fast, there's got to be a law about this somewhere. There's just got to be.

COP 1:   Well, sir, it is against the law to steal.

COP 2:   And assault . . .

VICE COP: Not that, her.

COP 1:   There's no law about looking that ugly, sir.

COP 2:   Come on, let's go.

VICE COP: No, she ain't going no where.

COP 1:   What are you talking about?

VICE COP: There's got to be a law about this down at central.

COP 1:   What is he talking about?

COP 2:   Why ask?

VICE COP: I'm talking about her.

COP 1:   What about her? . . . she's the complainant.

VICE COP: I'm talking about, what I'm talking about . . .

BOY 1:   What you rappin' about?

VICE COP: None of your business.

BOY 2:   You heard the man, none of your B.I. business, man. Now, keep tight before you get both of our asses kicked, man!

COP 1:   Shut up.

VICE COP: Don't tell me to shut up.

COP 2:   He didn't mean you, he meant them.

BOY 2:   Man, you gonna get us in big trouble with your big mouth, man.

VICE COP: He can speak for himself.

COP 1:   Yeah, I meant them, Jesus!

VICE COP: Now, what I'm talking about is as simple as this.

COP 1:   This hasn't been simple, believe me.

WOMAN: Talk straight, will you?

BOY 1:   He speak with fork tongue.

WOMAN: They all speak with fork tongue.

BOY 2:   Man, if they beat up on me, I'm gonna brain you, bro.

BOY 1:   Boy, you ain't doing nothing to me.

BOY 2:   We'll see about that.

COP 1:   You two can fight at the precinct. We got some gloves.

BOY 1:   That cool with me.

BOY 2:   Not with me. I ain't no prize fighter, man.

BOY 1:   No, man, you's a punk who talk much shit.

COP 1:   Shut up, all of yous, please. Now, sir, what is it with this woman?

VICE COP: What I'm talking about is simple.

COP 2:   You already said that. I'm still confused.

VICE COP: Yes, well, what I mean is . . . what I'm trying to say is that, can't you understand that there is something wrong here. I mean, well, that is, that er . . . er . . . er . . . that . . . I think that I mean I feel that there is something wrong here. Don't you see it. I mean it's perfectly clear to me. Can you see it?

COP 1:   To tell the truth . . . no . . .

VICE COP: That's why you're a transit cop working the graveyard shift.

COP 1:   I resent that.

VICE COP: Big deal, you resent the truth.

COP 1:   I'm taking them in.

VICE COP: No, wait, you can't. There's something wrong here and it has to be straightened out imme-

COP 1:   diately . . . I mean how can you let her get away with this crime.

COP 1:   What crime are you talking about?

WOMAN: Crime? I didn't commit no crime. What are you talking about, mister? You better make yourself clear before I sue you for false accusation. I didn't commit no crime. The crime was committed on me, mister. Now, get that right in your head.

COP 2:   She's right.

BOY 1:   What about us?

BOY 2:   What about us?

COP 1:   If you guys don't shut the fuck up, I'm going to smack the living shit out of you.

COP 2:   Hold it. . . . hold it, not here.

WOMAN: Just let me at them. . . .

COP 2:   Calm down, everybody, calm down. Please, let's get down to the bottom of this. Please explain yourself, officer, and please make it as brief and as clear as you possibly can. Thank you.

COP 1:   Yes, please.

BOY 1:   Hey, man, keep that monster cool.

BOY 2:   Be cool, bro, be cool. Please, I just got a cap on my teeth, bro, and if they knock it out, my old man is gonna kill me.

BOY 1:   Yeah, okay, bro?

VICE COP: Man, if we let her out of here without arresting her, we're all gonners for sure . . . don't you see that?

COP 1:   No.

WOMAN: He's crazy.

COP 2:   Lady, please . . .

WOMAN: He's crazy, he's insane, out of his motherfucking mind!

VICE COP: If we let her get away with this, who knows what will happen next.

COP 2:   What will happen to what . . . to who . . . what are you talking about?

COP 1:   Oh, let's not start on that again, please. Let's keep it clear.

COP 2:   You mean it's clear to you?

COP 1:   No . . .

COP 2:   What will happen to what? Let's start there.

VICE COP: To our society, man, to our society. What do you think I was trying to tell you all the time? What will happen to our society if we allow this woman to walk out of this men's toilet free without charging her with something . . . something that we can stick on her. Let's think . . . let's put our heads together.

COP 1:   I wonder if your head is together.

COP 2:   How long you been on the vice squad?

VICE COP: Peeping tomasina . . . that's it, peeping tomasina. There must be a law like that somewhere in the books downtown . . .

COP 1:   About a woman in the man's toilet?

COP 2:   You got to be kidding.

COP 1:   I don't think he is.

COP 2:   You're serious?

VICE COP: Of course, I'm serious.

COP 1:   He's serious.

VICE COP: You better believe that I'm serious. What will become of society if we allow things like this to go unpunished? What? Tell me what? Men in women's toilets . . . women in men's toilets . . . next thing we know, women will be in men's toilets standing up taking a piss. Can you imagine that, can you? No, but I can.

COP 1:   I bet you can.

VICE COP: You bet I can. I been working this beat long enough to know all the perverted thoughts and actions that take place in people's minds. I know them all . . . but I'm, strong, I stick to my guns . . . women standing up taking a piss, men sitting down . . . it can turn your stomach just thinking of it . . .

COP 2:   I'll try not to.

VICE COP: You take this as a joke, but you are not realizing the seriousness of it. What will become of our children, our children, our beautiful boys and girls? They'll be in a constant identity crisis. What will become of your daughter, if she walks into a toilet and finds a man putting on a sanitary napkin, what? . . . or your son, if he walks into the john and there's this stupid looking broad with one leg up in the air taking a piss? Think about things like that and you'll see the seriousness of it . . . think about it for one minute.

COP 1:   I did . . . we're leaving.

VICE COP: That's only the better part of the signs, for the worst is yet to come.

COP 1:   I did . . . we've leaving.

VICE COP: That's only the better part of the signs, for the worst is yet to come.

COP 1:   Repeat that.

VICE COP: I said that ain't all. There's more to be imagined . . . if we let this . . . this pervert go . . . what about the signs?

COP 1:   Signs, what signs?

VICE COP: The signs on the doors.

COP 2:   There are also other signs that one should take heed to, if you know what I mean.

VICE COP: Yes, I do.

COP 2:   You do?

VICE COP: Of course, I do. I understand everything there is to understand, but do you understand about the signs on the doors? The signs on the doors that indicate whether it's a men's room or a ladies' room . . . kings and queens . . . caballeros and caballeras . . . those signs on the toilet doors that are the most important thing that has come out of a civilized society, that's what. No . . . no, sir, not me. I am not taking part in this communist conspiracy to rid our society of the men and women signs on the toilet doors . . . not me, I am a true spirit of the revolution . . . long live Betsy Ross.

Man 4 enters.

VICE COP: Hold it, hold it, right there . . .
MAN 4:   *(In high feminine voice.)* Who me? . . . *(In husky voice.)* I mean, who me?
VICE COP: Yeah, you come 'ere.
MAN 4:   Yeah, what can I do for you? Good evening, officers . . . come on, I ain't got all day.
VICE COP: Hold it, I'm a police officer, too.
MAN 4:   Is he?
VICE COP: Why you ask them . . . don't you believe me . . . don't I look like a cop to you?
MAN 4:   No.
VICE COP: No?
COP 1:   That's why you're a detective.
COP 2:   Detectives are not supposed to look like cops.
VICE COP: Yeah, but everybody I know knows when a detective is around.
BOY 1:   Everybody I know knows too.
MAN 4:   Look, I wanna take a leak. Is there something wrong about that?
VICE COP: Don't be a wise guy . . . wasn't you in here before? Didn't I chase you out of here before?

31

MAN 4:   Me . . . hell, no. Why would I be chased out of a men's toilet for? That makes no sense to me.

COP 2:   Welcome to the club.

MAN 4:   Now, what can I do for you . . . officer?

VICE COP: Nothing, nothing at all . . . it's just that you . . . you look so familiar.

MAN 4:   Ain't never seen you before in my life.

VICE COP: Yeah, well, you better come back later or go to another toilet.

MAN 4:   Listen, I paid a quarter to get in here to take a leak.

VICE COP: There is police business going on in here . . . so you better turn around right now and leave.

MAN 4:   Police business in a subway toilet?

VICE COP: What makes you think that the law ends at subway toilet doors . . . in a toilet, even in a toilet the long arm of the law does not rest for one minute . . . and in here in this very toilet, mister, there is urgent police matters being taken care of, matters that may affect the future of our great democratic nation . . .

MAN 4:   Is he serious?

COP 1:   I think so.

WOMAN: He's crazy . . . call a cop, will ya, this man is crazy.

VICE COP: Shut up, you pervert, expounding communist . . .

MAN 4:   Yes, well, good night, officers . . . *(In a high feminine voice.)* good night, honey . . . byeee.

VICE COP: It's him, that lousy faggot. I knew it was him. I just knew it. I bet he's part of her group. They all are . . . I am putting this woman under arrest . . . come on, lady, let's go. Put out your hands, you degenerate . . . pinko bulldyke.

MAN 1:   Hello, God bless America, can I have my pants, please?

VICE COP: Are you making fun of me, mister? You better watch your step . . . if you wanna stay out of trouble, keep it clean.

WOMAN: Get your hands off me, you crazy honky . . . get them off me. Ain't you gonna help?!!

VICE COP: She is under arrest.

BOY 1:   Right on, put her in the same cell with us.

COP 1:   Shut up, punk.

COP 2:   What we going to do?

VICE COP: She is under arrest. Now, either of you can take the collar. It's a credit. I'll share it with you . . . you can have an assist.

COP 1:   No, you can have it by yourself.

COP 2:   Yeah, you can have it. After all, you pointed the violation out to us, didn't you?

VICE COP: Yes, but I am willing to give you credit.

COP 1:   No thanks.

COP 2:   Yeah, thanks, but no thanks . . . let's go . . .

COP 1:   Come on, boys, on the move . . .

COP 1:   Take her, she's yours.

WOMAN: This nut is arresting me?

COP 2:   Don't worry about it, lady, you have to go to the station, anyway, don't you? Well, this way you go in his car.

COP 1:   And under his care . . .

VICE COP: *(Singing.)* "God bless America, land of the free . . . etc . . ."

The woman begins to fight and curse him out.

COP 1:   All right, let's take them downtown.

COP 2:   Downtown? The station is uptown.

COP 1:   Yeah, I know, but it sounds more dramatic to say

downtown. "Okay, the game's over let's go downtown, we're booking you."

COP 2:   After him, I can see what you mean . . .

They exit with all the people under arrest and protesting their innocence.

Silence.

Man 1:   Hey, is there anybody out there? Hello, this is a
           man in trouble . . . is there anybody there? . . .
           shit . . . shit . . . shit . . .

Silence.

MAN 1:   Help . . . .help . . . helpppppppppppppp . . .

Curtain.

Cold Beer

Cold Beer

The People in the Play

MIKE:	*Beer-bellied poet.*
MELE:	*His spacey girlfriend.*
COP:	*Shiny, proud, CHIPS-type.*
MAN:	*Traveling salesman type.*
SMILES:	*Suburban, California-tanned teenager.*
LEGS:	*Suburban, California-tanned teenager.*

It's hot, Sunday, late afternoon, August in the year 1978. A young-looking, middle-aged, bearded, beerbelly poet sits on a wicker chair on a porch in the Echo Park district of East Los Angeles. He is surrounded by a swamp of cigarette butts and Bukowski books, with Tom Waits playing in the background. He wears a purple hat with broken ace-duce-tray on his head. He is shirtless, shoeless and wears faded blue jeans. There are pots with dying plants to keep him company, as well as one of those portable take-to-the-beach iceboxes filled with Budweiser beer at a lazy reach from his right hand. At his left is a small table with two unopened packs of Pall Malls and an almost dead bottle of J & B next to an out-of-place modern red telephone. In front of him is a Purina checkboard coffee table with a 1940 black Smith-Corona portable typewriter devouring a blank 8" by 11" white sheet of paper devoted to driving a writer insane. Mike chain smokes and chain drinks his beer. Both are part of his poetic image, for Mike is a poet-writer and is infected with that rare germ of insanity once the deluxe privilege allotted only to the rich and famous, but America is coming of age and now even poor slobs like Mike can stake claim to it. With this degree hanging over him like a halo, Mike takes leaks off the porch into the neighbor's driveway and loves to soak their poodle . . .

VOICE: Poopoo . . . oooh, Poopoo, you stink of piss . . . how in heaven's name do you always come in at this time smelling like a skid row bum? Oooh, Poopoo . . .

MIKE: *(Mimicking.)* Ooh Poopoo . . . Poopoo . . . how the hell can any decent dog-loving person give a name like that to any living thing? That's simply unnatural cruelty. *(Picks up the phone.)* Hello . . . ASPCA . . . yeah, my name's Mike Poor . . . yeah, listen, I wanna report cruelty to an animal . . . call who? . . . the Humane Society, for the what? . . . Look, these people next door have this dog . . . no, they don't beat him . . . yeah, they feed it, in fact, the mother eats better than me . . . what? Oh, well, they gave the poor miserable slob a name like Poopoo. I mean, ain't there something you can do about that? . . . Hello . . . up yours too . . . *(Hangs up.)*

Mike goes back to his chain-smoking, chain-drinking mode of living. Mele, a female friend of Mike's comes out to the porch wearing an Indian shirt made in Korea, old jeans cut to the pockets. She is shoeless and smoking a fat joint.

MELE: Whacha doin'?

MIKE: Looking at this thing here.

MELE: Poor thing.

MIKE: Poor thing?

MELE: It looks so lonely.

MIKE: How do you think it makes me feel?

MELE: You wanna toke?

MIKE: Naw . . . I'm trying to create.

MELE: You wanna toke?

MIKE: Yeah, maybe it'll help me bring profound thoughts into the printed word, opening the door to immortality . . .

MELE: Oh, wow . . . that sounds profound.

MIKE: Yeah, it docs, doesn't it? *(He types.)*

MELE: I like the way you type.

MIKE: How about the way I write?

MELE: I like the way you type.

MIKE: Thanks . . .

MELE: I mean you just don't sit straight up with your ass touching the back of the chair like a row of legal secretaries . . . you got movement . . . rhythm . . . you type like a song being sung in one of those Humphrey Bogart movies . . .

39

MIKE: Bogart, huh?

MELE: Just your typing . . .

MIKE: How about my writing?

MELE: You type nice . . .

MIKE: You're a very committed person, aren't ya?

MELE: I support women's rights . . . gay rights . . . skyhorse and Mohawk . . . legalization of mari- juana . . . prostitution . . .

MIKE: And my typing . . .

MELE: Yeah, your typing is cool . . .

MIKE: You make me wanna go back to longhand.

MELE: I can't comment on your longhand.

MIKE: Forget it . . . *(Phone rings and Mike answers.)* It's your dime and my time. Start talking. Oh, hi, Patrick . . . what? Oh yeah, man I'm right on the writing . . . it's got movement, rhythm . . . it's cool . . . you wanna ask Mele? No, I'm on the case like Sam the Spade . . . Later . . . Pat thinks I'm lazy . . . he likes my writing . . . but he thinks I'm lazy . . .

MELE: How about your typing?

MIKE: He thinks it stinks . . .

MELE: He got no class.

MELE: Thanks.

MELE: I'm going to the store. Ya want something?

MIKE: Yeah, another six pack.

MELE: Bye . . .

MIKE: At least I got rhythm . . .

Mike enters the house and we hear him put Latin music on the record player. He comes back to his restful place. A black and white pulls up. A young L.A.'s finest steps up to the porch. He walks as if he's the second-coming-of Gary Cooper in "High Noon."

COP: Ya live 'ere?

MIKE: I sleep . . . shit . . . eat here . . . Living, that's another matter. Life is not just resting your head. Life . . .

COP: What are ya, a wisenheimer?

MIKE: No, I'm a poor . . .

COP: Lady next door says you keep pissing on her dog . . . that right?

MIKE: She should give the dog another name.

COP: What?

MIKE: She calls him Poopoo.

COP: Poopoo? What kinda name is that?

MIKE: French I think.

COP: Those French are weird.

MIKE: Ever been to France?

COP: When I was in the army. They sure are one bunch of prejudiced creeps . . . they don't even speak English. I see all the police stories on T.V., all the detective movies, but I won't go see the "Pink Panther." It's French.

MIKE: I thought Peter Sellers was English.

COP: He is?

MIKE: Think so . . . ya wanna beer?

COP: Thanks, but no thanks . . . watching my belly.

MIKE: Women say waist.

COP: Yeah, well . . . I warned ya about pissing on, whacha ya say his name is?

MIKE: Poopoo.

COP: Jesus . . . that's cruel.

MIKE: Yeah, I tried telling that to the A.S.P.C.A. They tole me to shove it.

COP: Creeps . . . lousy creeps . . . Poopoo, Jesus! Listen, stop pissing on Poopoo.

MIKE: Ya want a megaphone?

COP: Just want her to know I'm doing my job . . . what ya do, mister, for a living, that is?

MIKE: I'm a poet . . .
COP: A communist, huh? . . . Well, if this pissing on
         Poopoo is some kinda communist plot, you gonna
         be sorry . . . Poopoo, huh?
MIKE: Yes, poor Poopoo.
COP: Jesus, so long . . . Poopoo . . . cruel . . .

*Mike returns to his creative state of mind. A young Robert de
Niro type comes to him.*

MAN: Hi . . .
MIKE: Hi.
MAN: You know who lives there?
MIKE: You from the police?
MAN: No.
MIKE: Internal Revenueeee?
MAN: No . . . nor from the FBI or CIA or
         Watergate . . . I'm looking for a friend of mine?
MIKE: Poopoo?
MAN: What?
MIKE: Poopoo lives next door.
MAN: Sounds French.
MIKE: I piss on him a lot.
MAN: The French like that kinda thing. I'm looking for
         an Italian guy.
MIKE: You're from the Mafia.
MAN: Name's Guy Santini.
MIKE: Poopoo lives there and that place is vacant . . .
         state won't rent it out.
MAN: Nice place . . . too bad . . .
MIKE: Yeah, I like to take craps in there at night. I like to
         take craps in haunted houses . . . sometimes I jack
         off in there . . .
MAN: You piss on Poopoo, huh?
MIKE: Yep . . .

42

MAN:	He should go down Santa Monica Blvd.
MIKE:	They take him to Griffith Park.
MAN:	That's a nice place . . . oh, by the way, can you use a good blowjob?
MIKE:	Everyone can use a good blowjob.
MAN:	I'm a pro . . . not like the suckers. Some people say I got a tambourine tongue.
MIKE:	No kidding?
MAN:	Yeah, I developed this technique with my tongue . . . I'm the greatest.
MIKE:	I type with rhythms.
MAN:	I got these movements.
MIKE:	I type with movement . . .
MAN:	I dig beerbelly truck drivers. Are you a truck driver?
MIKE:	No, I'm a beerbelly poet.
MAN:	Any good?
MIKE:	I type good . . .
MAN:	So, would you like a dynamite blowjob?
MIKE:	You sound like a used car salesman, except you ain't got Foster Grant wraparounds . . .
MAN:	I left them in the car. I work for Worthingford . . . I can even give a blowjob standing on my head.
MIKE:	Got to try it sometime . . .
MAN:	You sure you don't want a terrific blowjob?
MIKE:	You wanna beer?
MAN:	No, watching my waist . . .
MIKE:	Sorry . . . I'm creating.
MAN:	Well, it's your loss.
MIKE:	Can't win them all.
MAN:	Bye, now . . . I just love that beerbelly. You sure you ain't a truck driver?
MIKE:	No . . . sorry . . . bye . . .
MAN:	Oh well, . . . if you don't advertise, you don't sell.

MIKE: Hello, America . . .

No sooner is the Robert de Niro type gone than Mike hears two young voices. Two bronze, tan blonde-haired kids in their early teens call to him. It's only up close that Mike defines them to be boys. They wear sandles and cut off jeans. One smiles a lot . . . the other keeps smoothing imaginary dust or lotion on his beauty-contest-winning legs.

SMILES: Hey, mister . . . hey, man, you know the guy that lives down there?
LEGS: See him, the one with the blue-towel bathrobe on?
MIKE: Yeah . . . nice old man, used to be a good gardener, I think.
SMILES: Can I have a beer?
LEGS: Can I have a smoke?
MIKE: Help yourselves.
SMILES: Hey man, that man is weird.
LEGS: Yeah man, out of it.
SMILES: He went out to lunch and never came back.
MIKE: You got nice legs.
SMILES: That's what he said.
LEGS: Yeah?
MIKE: Ain't no crime in using the same line.
LEGS: I do, don't I? Do a lot of running and knee bends, ride the bicycle a lot too.
SMILES: What do you do?
MIKE: I'm a poet.
SMILES: Oh, sweet Jesus, another fairy.
MIKE: Can you fight?
SMILES: What?
MIKE: Can you fight good enough to whip my ass?
SMILES: No . . . you're older.
MIKE: Poet . . .
SMILES: What?

LEGS: He's saying if you can't fight, you better call him poet.

MIKE: Son, I stand five-foot-six, weight: 155pounds, got ten inches of dick, four pounds of balls. You best care who you call fairy.

SMILES: I like that . . . can you say it again?

MIKE: He's got nice legs.

SMILES: That's what the old man said.

LEGS: Yeah, I was riding me and him, picking up empty soda bottles to get the deposit . . . making some bread.

SMILES: Yeah, and this old man down there calls us, starts talking to us, then asks what we're doing.

LEGS: . . . all the time eyeing my legs . . . made me feel weird.

SMILES: Looking directly at my lips . . .

MIKE: He liked your smile.

LEGS: Then he says, you wanna make some quick cash . . . so we say, sure, what we got to do? He says, help me clean the car garage. We say, yeah, man, sure. . . .

SMILES: We start to go into the place, he puts his hands on me.

LEGS: Yeah, then he comes to me and swipes my legs, like if they was made of china.

MIKE: You got nice legs.

SMILES: Can I have another beer?

MIKE: No, you got to watch your belly.

SMILES: I'll pay for it.

MIKE: In that case, help yourselves.

LEGS: Anyway, we go in, he follows us in, we move a couple things around.

SMILES: I saw him first.

LEGS: He was naked . . .

SMILES: Naked . . . pure naked . . .

MIKE: Most of us are born that way.

LEGS: Yeah, man, naked and he was jacking off, right there in front of us . . .

SMILES: . . . and it wasn't even hard.

MIKE: You noticed, huh?

SMILES: What's that got to do with anything?

MIKE: Nothing.

LEGS: Anyway, I got scared.

SMILES: Not me, I'd killed him if he came near me . . .

MIKE: Did he?

LEGS: No, he just stood by the corner looking at my legs, jerking off, man, that was weird.

SMILES: Then his wife came in and started screaming at him and yelling that she was going to tell his son . . . oh, man, we ran out of there.

LEGS: Hey, there he is . . . they're putting him in that car. Look, he's still jacking off . . . wow crazy . . . wow.

MIKE: How does his wife look?

LEGS: Ugly.

SMILES: No teeth.

MIKE: You got nice legs.

SMILES: I got great teeth, helps my smile.

MIKE: Yeah, you do . . . get any money?

LEGS: Naw . . . man . . . nothing, he gyped us.

MIKE: Bad investment . . .

SMILES: Yeah, a bum trip . . . you want anything worked on around here? Your plants are all dying.

LEGS: Telephones ringing.

MIKE: Never answer the phone when I'm creating.

SMILES: How about it, mister?

MIKE: No, thanks, I jacked off this morning.

LEGS: Let's go.

SMILES: Bye . . .

LEGS: This guy is just as weird as the man down there.

SMILES: I think he's cool . . .
MIKE: I type cool . . . bye . . .
SMILES: Can I get another beer?
MIKE: No.
SMILES AND LEGS: Bye . . .

Mele drives up . . . pours the beer in the box.

MELE: What they want?
MIKE: Attention.   *(Phone rings again.)* Oh, hi
         Patrick . . . yeah, man, I got it down . . . it's got
         movement . . . rhythm . . . the typing is cool, it's
         got legs . . . and smiles and cops and pissing on
         Poopoo . . . gives you a tambourine job . . .
         heavy, I'll bring it in about 3. By the way, Pat, you
         think you can give me cash . . . I ain't got a bank
         account to cash a check . . . no, man, I ain't got
         no identity . . . lost my wallet . . . yep . . .
         thanks, man . . .
MELE: So, what's been happening?
MIKE: Oh, nothing . . . hey, you heard they're thinking
         of dropping neutron bombs on the South Bronx?
MELE: Wow!
MIKE: Hey, check it out . . . you see, the government
         drops the neutron bombs on the South Bronx as a
         solution to the people problem there . . . then they
         give out these CETA jobs to the kids from Harlem
         to clean up the bodies . . . and some guys put out
         a grant application to NEA to study the creative
         process of neutron dying . . . and then . . .
MELE: I like your typing.
MIKE: There's this old man who jerks off a lot . . .

*Typing can be heard all over the Echo Park district of Los
Angeles that night . . . with Tom Waits in the background:
"warm beer and cold women / I just don't fit in, etc."*

The Guntower

The Guntower

People in the Play:

German Rosado
Simmon Johnson

The play takes place in the guntower of one of America's prisons.

It's the morning shift. Simmon Johnson is pacing the tower, bored to death. Every ten minutes or so he turns the handle on a box on the wall. He does this automatically. There is a faint sound of guitar and harmonica music being played, but not together to make a tune. There's the sound of basketballs hitting the concrete and people talking, a lot of people.

SIMMON: Hey . . . hey . . . yeah, you, stupid . . . you jive ass nigger, why ya let that sap steal the ball from under ya? . . . ya . . . ya . . . don't open your mouth to run no excuses now. Shit, my baby sister can play better. Yeah, she's only three. No wonder you in the joint . . .

VOICE: Ahhh, go on Mr. Johnson, ya rap all that fly shit up there on the rodhouse, but on the ground you's a chump.

SIMMON: Your mom's a chump . . . and don't forget that you are talking to a correctional officer of this here state, boy . . . just 'cause you saw my shoes under ya mama's bed, don't mean that we are related, boy.

VOICE: Pick up on this Correctional Officer, Simmon Johnson, sir.

SIMMON: Shit, I can see why you play like a sissy. Ya mami was ya daddy and you know what you can do with that thing, if it's long enough . . . in fact, I'm getting off here to head toward the messhall before you get there.

VOICE: What about the messhall? Speak up, son, I can't year ya.

SIMMON: I said that they're serving franks today and I want to have yours cut before you take them back to the cell . . . shit, you wanna play the dozens with me, boy? I played the dozens before you could talk. Shit, if I ever told ya how to play, shit, it may just blow away that split pea of a brain.

VOICE: If I told ya who I wanna play with, ya might just get mad enough to shoot me, brotherrr.

SIMMON: Ain't nothing that serious, brotherrr.

VOICE: Ya all right, then . . . later . . .

SIMMON: Ya okay . . . later . . . take it easy . . . you too, brotherman. Hey, git off his ass . . . didn't know ya went that way, brother . . . *(Goes back to pacing the tower.)* I wish these motherfuckers would stop looking at me like if I were some freak or something . . . motherfuckers, close your fucking eyes . . . if I pick my nose and wipe the snots on my clothes, you laugh at me. If I scratch my ass, you yell that that's digging for oil. I bet that you would like to get my lollipop and squeeze it hard on your tongue, wouldn't you? But, dig on this, suckers. Put your head on an acid mood so you can listen to the silence that's within ya loud assholes. If you had done that, you might not have been here today . . . assholes . . . assholes.

VOICE: ASSHOLES, that's what you are in there, assholes . . . so get that straight. I am a big prick and you are a bunch of assholes . . . and I would like to fuck every asshole in here. Do you understand, assholes? So, if you don't wanna be fucked by a big prick like me, assholes, you better get every thing done on the double. Is that right, assholes? Louder, asshokes. I can't hear you, assholes. Remember that good, you fucking assholes. This is not boot camp. This is the real thing out here and out here if you play pussy, you get fucked by a mean prick and there's plenty of mean pricks out

53

there in them bushes looking for assholes to fuck. You hear me? Now I asked for some real men and they send me you assholes and you assholes are going to have to learn to be pricks, unless you wanna get fucked. Fight or fuck, that's the motto of this squad. Do you read me? Well, answer up loud enough that they can hear you in the North. I don't want them to know that a lot of assholes are going to be fighting them. I want them to fear the pricks that I throw out that way, right? Right now let's see what you assholes know about your women. Asshole, your woman is your rifle, stupid . . . it's not a laughing matter out in that bush. You read me, assholes? Okay, assholes, get ready to move out into the way of the almighty prick. Move, assholes, on the fucking double, on the fucking double, you chicken-livered shitheads. Get that lead out of your fucking ass, assholes. Move on the fucking double . . . don't think, act . . . don't think, do as you are told . . . you stupid assholes, you have no time to think out here . . . you either act or you die. Don't think, assholes, don't think, you fucking assholes . . . there's a prick coming your way, assholes, get out of the way or get fucked . . . it's hot out here, motherfuckers, and I don't wanna be bothered by your asshole mistakes. You understand, assholes?

SIMMON: Yeah, man, it sure was hot out there in the bush. It was hot in more ways than one, what with this fucking Louey out of the school running all this asshole bullshit on us, like it was the first time I ever been out in the bush. So what if it was the first time out there for me and the rest of the fellas? We were going to waste him in the first fire fight we got into. He was going and that was for

54

sure. It was hot and all those bugs and people on you all the time, not knowing when or how the end will come for you, that that's the way it is, that's the real way it is, the bush slapping you in the face all the time, the sun beating on the top of your helmet all the time, the death traps entering in your fears all the time, and you never get a fucking break from any of them. The motherfuckers are going to get wasted the first time I get one in my sights. Man, shit, it's hot out here. Never knew any place on earth could be blood brother to the sun, man. The earth and the sun must be related somehow . . . else why would it be so fucking hot out here, man? There is the clearing. We are going into the village . . . there's only old men and women around, some little kids peeing, some taking shits . . . cows . . . birds and shit. There's nothing out there. There's nothing here. No. Gonzalez, don't fuck with that fireplace . . . oh, shit, don't move, Gonzalez . . . medic, Gonzalez hit a trap, he hit a trap. Chin Chow is hit. There's a sniper around down on the fucking floor, a sniper . . . where . . . where . . . there . . . in the hut, in the fucking hut, there's a sniper in the fucking hut. Set up the light machine gun . . . mortar . . . mortar . . . set up that fucking light machine gun on the fucking double, you stupid motherfucker. You got us in this motherfucking mess. Move, incoming mail . . . down . . . down . . . get your fucking head down, Lunbrosky . . . oh, shit, his head is gone . . . down, watch the sniper . . . you fucking grade-A asshole, you a big prick. You're the fucking asshole . . . frag the Louey now . . . get him, get this fucking prick out of the way, assholes, are we . . . you fucking goldbrick nigger, spray that fucking hut, spray that fucking hut. The sniper is in the fucking hut. Down, mother, mortar . . . spray the fucking hut . . . the hut, the hut, you idiot, the fucking hut. Spray that fucking hut . . . cover me . . . cover me, plenty of fire. I want plenty of fire. Spray the fucking cover. I wanna get in a grenade, motherfuckers. Give me plenty of fire cover . . . hold it . . . grenade . . . boom . . . ah . . . ah . . . now, motherfucker, come out . . . she came out of there running, holding the body of a headless baby . . . hit her, hit her, waste that old fucking bitch . . . there's a bomb in the baby, there's got to be a bomb in the baby . . . oh, my god . . . so I picked up my gun and I . . . I . . . I . . . did what I had to do . . . I hit the gook . . . you fucking no good for nothing gooks, you killed my buddy Gonzalez . . . slanthead motherfuckers, you gave him no chance to be out here long enough to get a fucking piece of gook pussy . . . wasted the bitch . . . my stomach is turning and all the shit is coming out of my head . . . it's supposed to come out through my asshole, not out of my mouth. It tastes nasty, my throat feels like a giant shit bowl . . . raattaaa raattaaaa, motherfucker, raatttaaaa, motherfucker, you old bitch, who told you to be in the fucking hut with your baby. Who told you to know me. I'm not responsible for your life, bitch. You did it to yourself, not me, not Uncle Sam. You did it to yourself, bitch. You did it. Stop looking at me with your dead eyes, bitch. I'll pluck them out . . . I'll pluck them out and bury them so that you can stop looking at me with those dead eyes . . . stop it . . . fuck you guys. I don't want her staring at me like if I caused her death. I didn't. You guys saw what happened. Even the lieutenant got it. Should he get a medal? His mother will be proud of him. He died in combat, in combat just like she died in combat. But not Gonzalez, he died like a fool . . . his head blown half way off. Look at all those flies eating at him already. Man, he must taste good to them or they may be just another product of this piece of earth, starving. Food . . . food is what they see in him. Gonzalez, my lover . . . I'll bury your eyes, bitch. I'll take his tag . . . get the fuck away from him. I'll take his tag home for him, but this bitch will never, not even in her hell, will she see. I'm burning her eyes . . . bitch . . . where is the head of the baby, where is it? Get it for me. I want to take a picture to send home to mother. Here, throw me his head, just like a baseball. Here, take my picture . . . stop it . . . stop it. Nooo.

GERMAN: Hey, hey.

SIMMON: What ya want?

SIMMON: What the fuck you screaming at me for?

GERMAN: Cuz you started screaming at me, that's why.

SIMMON: What the fuck do you want, anyway? The post is off limits even to you, Rosado, . . . beat it. What are you doing out here, anyway? You ain't the meal runner. So you have no business here. Look, I'm not that gung-ho. You know that, Rosado. But this post is off limits and if you don't leave these grounds, I'm gonna have to write you up.

GERMAN: Look, man, I got orders from the dep to come here.

SIMMON: For what?

GERMAN: To report for duty. If it's a mistake . . . but I don't think it is, considering the rumor I . . .

SIMMON: I don't wanna hear about any rumors and, what orders? Let me see them. Look, they didn't inform me on any orders about you coming here. Why didn't they inform me?

GERMAN: Look, I'm only a guard here . . . and I ain't been here long enough that they would call me into the brass office and let me know confidential information. You know, I just got off probationary period.

SIMMON: Put your orders in the basket.

GERMAN: What are you talking about, man? This ain't the fucking army.

SIMMON: What do you know about the fucking army?

GERMAN: Look, man, they just tole me to come out here, that's all.

SIMMON: Well, I don't know why they would tell you something like that, because it said in the book that there is only one man to a tower, unless there's an emergency and I don't know of any emergency around here.

GERMAN: Man, why don't you call the fucking deputy superintendent and cut out all these bullshit hassles?

SIMMON: I'll do just that . . . and I would appreciate it if you stop cursing so motherfucking much.

GERMAN: Call the fucking, dep, will ya? Or else I'll leave and let you deal with the fucking brass and I'll do all the fucking cursing that I want. I'm a fucking grown man, Mister Johnson. Understand that now. Don't let my face fool you.

SIMMON: Your face is a fool.

GERMAN: Well, are you gonna call or are you going to let me in there?

SIMMON: Just wait a fucking minute, okay? I'm calling the D.S.O. Hello, sarge, can I speak with the dep?

No . . . nothing personal . . . oh . . . yeah, well, sorry . . . sarge, if it's not personal . . . speak to you first . . . yeah, sarge, I got it, sir . . . well, there's a guy named Rosado here . . . no, sir, he's outside . . . yes, sir, right away . . . well, I wasn't informed that he was coming up here, sir. Well, no, I don't have any stripes, sir. No, I am not questioning the assignment, sir. The book states, sir . . . no, I don't always go by the book, just that this is a tower . . . yes, sir, I'll let him up immediately . . . right, goodbye. Okay, come on up . . . watch your step. Did you eat yet?

GERMAN: Yeah, thanks.
SIMMON: The meal runner will be around in a while, anyway.
GERMAN: Yeah, I know.
SIMMON: You keep a nice uniform.
GERMAN: So do you.
SIMMON: I try to.
GERMAN: Shoes are marine shined.
SIMMON: Yep.
GERMAN: Served in the Nam?
SIMMON: 23 months, 12 of them in the bush country.
GERMAN: Really?
SIMMON: You in the army?
GERMAN: Yep, Special Forces.
SIMMON: Wow, really!
GERMAN: Yep.
SIMMON: If I'd gone into the army, I would have chosen that, you know?
GERMAN: Yeah, I kinda like action, you know.
SIMMON: So do I.
GERMAN: How you like the job?
SIMMON: Pays okay. A lot of good benefits too.
GERMAN: Look, man, don't throw dagger stares at me,

man. I didn't ask to come up here, you know. I'm just a grunt like you, man. I have no say on the assignment of the day, you know, man. Like, be cool.

SIMMON: Ya right . . . I'm sorry man.

GERMAN: Look, man . . .

SIMMON: Hey, would you please cut that shit out.

GERMAN: What you talking 'bout? Look, man, I don't . . .

SIMMON: That. Just that. Stop saying "look, man" . . . "look, man" . . . that's . . . that's, well, just stop saying it.

GERMAN: Okay, that's no skin off my back.

SIMMON: Man, it's that after you're up here a while, you'll understand why it's not good to keep saying something over and over again and again.

GERMAN: That's a nice tie pin.

SIMMON: Thanks . . . a gift from a friend.

GERMAN: You get a lot of gifts from friends?

SIMMON: No, not really, about the same amount that you get.

GERMAN: Shit, I don't get any.

SIMMON: You must not have any friends.

GERMAN: Yeah.

SIMMON: Yeah? Yeah, you don't have any friends?

GERMAN: No . . . not that. I mean I have friends. Everybody has friends. Just that my friends don't give out gifts.

SIMMON: Really, is that a tradition among Puerto Ricans?

GERMAN: How the hell should I know about Puerto Ricans?

SIMMON: Just asking. Maybe you did know and I could have learned something.

GERMAN: Yeah, but I don't know.

SIMMON: You think that you ever will?
GERMAN: Sure, if I put my mind to it, it'll pop up just like that.
SIMMON: Just like that?
GERMAN: Just like that.
SIMMON: I don't believe you, just like that pop.
GERMAN: I see no reason why you shouldn't believe me. Have I ever lied to you before?
SIMMON: Well, no . . .
GERMAN: You see.
SIMMON: Well, that's because I never really spoke to you before.
GERMAN: That doesn't mean anything.
SIMMON: Of course, it does.
GERMAN: No, it doesn't. A lot of people never spoke to me.
SIMMON: Well, that's nothing new. I know a lot of people that I never met before too. I see them on the streets, in department stores, shopping . . . in the movies, at baseball games.
GERMAN: Who do you think will take the series this year?
SIMMON: The Mets, naturally, who else?
GERMAN: I thought the Cardinals might take it this year. They got a good pitching team for a back-up.
SIMMON: Naw . . . baseball is like . . . like boxing. Who ever has the strongest punch wins by a knock-out . . . see?
GERMAN: I don't know about that.
SIMMON: What's there to know?
GERMAN: A whole lot. Don't you believe in that?
SIMMON: Of course, I do.
GERMAN: Oh, for a moment there I thought you be different in that.
SIMMON: No, not me. I was raised Protestant.

GERMAN: I was baptised a Roman Catholic.

SIMMON: So what?

GERMAN: That's what I always say: so what.

SIMMON: I mean, we both believe in the Lord.

GERMAN: J.C.?

SIMMON: He for me. *(Pause.)* So, you don't have any friends?

GERMAN: I have friends.

SIMMON: I thought you said that you didn't.

GERMAN: I have friends. It's just that I don't have any *friends.*

SIMMON: Oh, I see what you mean.

GERMAN: You do?

SIMMON: Sure, you said that you have friends, but that you don't have any friends to speak of.

GERMAN: Hey, you could be my friend.

SIMMON: I have to think about that first. You know, you just don't become somebody's friend just because somebody asks you to be their friend. You know, I mean, it takes time being somebody's friend.

GERMAN: That's why I have none. I don't have the time.

SIMMON: So, you say that Puerto Rican tradition can pop just like that in your mind, if you put your mind to it.

GERMAN: Yeah, man, just like that. You know that a bunch of centuries ago my people were dying and they knew that their whole civilization was being wasted. So what did they do? They all got together and transferred themselves out of this planet.

SIMMON: Get outta here with that bullshit, man. You expect me to believe that shit?

GERMAN: Well, it's true. It's in the history books.

SIMMON: I never read about it.

GERMAN: 'Cause you never came across it like I did.

SIMMON: You came across it in a book?

GERMAN: Yeah . . . in the library.

SIMMON: This up here is like a library.

GERMAN: It don't look like one.

SIMMON: Only because it doesn't have any walls about it.

GERMAN: Yeah, maybe you're right.

SIMMON: They just sat down and transferred themselves out of this planet? I don't believe it.

GERMAN: Well, you know they were very spiritual.

SIMMON: So are my people . . . black is beautiful.

GERMAN: Beautiful also are the souls of all my people.

SIMMON: That was said by a black man.

GERMAN: It was?

SIMMON: Yep, guy by the name of Langston Hughes . . . he lived in Harlem.

GERMAN: He's dead?

SIMMON: I think so.

GERMAN: Ain't that something. I thought I said that.

SIMMON: No, Langston Hughes said it first.

GERMAN: That don't even sound like a black man's name.

SIMMON: Well, it is . . . at least it was his name.

GERMAN: You read a lot of his things?

SIMMON: When I was a kid.

GERMAN: You don't read his things any more?

SIMMON: Naw, I study up here . . . I'm going to college.

GERMAN: Really, what for?

SIMMON: Well, I don't plan to be a correctional officer all my life, you know. I wanna do other things too.

GERMAN: There ain't much to do any more anyway.

SIMMON: That's what you think. You just ain't giving yourself the time. That's why you have no friends.

GERMAN: But I have a dog.

SIMMON: A hunting dog?

GERMAN: I don't hunt . . . can't stand to kill anything
            any more. The Nam was enough for me in the
            killing thing. Like it was fun killing there because
            you had a right to kill. You know what I mean? But
            then again, I don't know, maybe I'll get a gun and
            go hunting animals.

SIMMON: Remember, they put you in jail for hunting the
            two-legged kind.

GERMAN: Wow, you really get to see the whole play
            from here. I mean, like you really get to see the
            whole thing. Look at that view . . . wow . . . hey,
            Simmon Johnson, looka that. Look, you can see
            the whole play. Wow, nice, really nice . . . look at
            them idiots over there looking at us . . . look at
            them looking at us. They sure have a lot of nerve,
            man . . . they sure do . . . they're probably talk-
            ing about us, calling us all kinds of pigs and shit
            like that, you know. Man, they're wasting their
            lives and they're talking about us. I feel like blow-
            ing the motherfuckers to pieces right off. I bet you
            that I could do it even from this distance, I could.
            Wasting their lives away looking like . . . like shit.
            That's pitiful shit over there, sitting down looking
            up here . . . I bet you . . . I bet you they wish
            they were up here and us down there . . . but it's
            not like that because they have no guts to make it
            up here. But I bet you they wish they had the heart
            and the guts to be up here dealing with life and
            lives like we are, right? Goddamn right. I'm right,
            shit, I know that. I'm right. Oh buddy, it sure feels
            great to be alive, don't it? Up here you know what
            it means to be alive, to be for real with whatever
            fantasy you want to be for real with, right? Yeah,
            man, I know that you are getting pissed off at me

for being here, man, but remember I didn't make it happen: someone else did, someone else wrote the shit, someone else passed it on to me and I'm only acting it out, so don't blame me, man, blame the dude that wrote the fucking thing. He's the one to blame . . . like if you get bored just tell me and I'll shut up, be very quiet and you can return to that private world of yours. Hey, why not look at it this way? I am here to help you . . . okay . . . to help you look at that world that's sitting right in front of you and if you let your mind wander to the real truth, you'll see what beauty lies in front of you before you meet your death or before you go home to your bickering and daily routine of bills and headaches. Johnson, you have a great bunch of faces out there to look at . . . right through this scope I see many that I wouldn't mind shooting their wigs off . . . you know . . . look . . . am I interrupting what you have created in yourself? I'm sorry . . . but now that I'm here and you feel interrupted, you'll learn to appreciate your fantasy, plastic life of automat dinner parties . . . and when you enter that world and again you remember how much you missed it and you'll never neglect a piece of it again . . . right, Johnson?

SIMMON: What you want to eat?

GERMAN: Ham on rye, no mustard . . .

SIMMON: Anything to drink with it?

GERMAN: Root beer be fine with me, thanks.

SIMMON: What you got to pay for it?

GERMAN: You know something, I take it back.

SIMMON: Take what back?

GERMAN: Asking you to be my friend.

SIMMON: Why?

GERMAN: Because you couldn't be my friend, even if you wanted to.

65

SIMMON: What ya mean?

GERMAN: I mean even if you wanted to, you couldn't ever be my friend.

SIMMON: Why not?

GERMAN: Because I wouldn't let you.

SIMMON: Why wouldn't you let me be your friend? I want to be your friend.

GERMAN: Well, I don't want you to be, because you don't know enough.

SIMMON: Enough of what?

GERMAN: Of being what you are.

SIMMON: A black man?

GERMAN: No, a thing of power.

SIMMON: What power? There ain't no power up here.

GERMAN: You see, you don't ever realize that there is power up here. You can do anything and really get away with it. I mean, you have the power to create and the power to destroy when you are up here and that's why we can't be friends, because I know of the power and you don't.

SIMMON: Maybe you can teach me to be your friend.

GERMAN: Naw, can't teach an old dog new tricks.

SIMMON: That's being prejudiced.

GERMAN: No, it ain't.

SIMMON: Yes, it is.

GERMAN: It is? Really?

SIMMON: Yes, it is . . . you can be prejudiced to many things, not just skin color, my man. I don't want power, anyway. No, that's not true. I do want power . . . and control. We all do.

GERMAN: Yeah, but you already got it. That's why I don't think we should be friends.

SIMMON: Maybe you're right.

GERMAN: I know I'm right, you idiot. Don't you realize what you got up here, man. Don't you know what's up here with you every time you climb up here, man. Don't you know? Don't you understand the power you control up here? Every time you are up here looking down at the world . . . look at them looking at you . . . look at them looking at you helplessly, looking at you waiting to see what your next move is gonna be. Don't you know the strength that lies up here with you? . . . the power to control the lives of all those that are staring at you? There is enough power and control up here to fill the egos of every man staring at us. Up here is the doorstep to being a god . . . a creator of life. You see, you don't know them things, but I do. I realized it the first time I saw this place. The first time I saw it I said, that's where I want to be, because that's where the power to control lives is at . . . and I made it my business to get up here to check out if what I believed to be true is the truth . . . and it is. Check it out . . . man, check it out the way it's supposed to be checked out. I see more than any of those down there. Maybe I don't hear as much as those down there do, but who the fuck cares about hearing the damn thing anyway. It's seeing and feeling and smelling and tasting the fucking play in yourself. That's what counts, right? That's what counts. Nothing else does. I know because I made it my business to know all of it. You see, I can talk down to all of them out there. I can laugh down at them and all they can do is look up at me . . . look up to me . . . that's the power of being God . . . you don't believe that? Here, I'm God . . . you don't, huh? Okay, motherfucker, look at this. What is it? It's a gun, right? It kills man. It kills woman. It kills children. It kills whatever I point at. If it has

67

life, it will kill it. Now, do you believe what I am trying to tell you? Baby, you are God, and if you don't believe that I am too, don't bet your last breath on it. You see, God has a sense of humor as well as a sense of insanity. You sit there in the sun thinking that I'm crazy or something like that. You sit there thinking that I'm crazy, right? But, man, I ain't crazy. There's nothing wrong with me, nothing at all. I am God on earth. I put this gun to your head and you don't know if I really loaded the fucking thing or not. You don't know if I loaded the fucking thing, right? You say to yourself, "is this a fucking play that this sucker is doing or is he for real with that thing?" Remember that dude in Texas up in the tower of the university? He went up there and he was God. He took the lives of many people. And now I may take your life, because I feel like I got the power to do so and get away with it. I point this gun out there and everybody sits calm. But if I were to pull this trigger and somebody's head blew away, then I'd be considered insane, unless I say I didn't know what happenned to me up here. I just became like that dude in Texas. Remember him? And if you saw me smile and blow the head off one of those people out there, you would know what I am talking about, right? And they would scream in fear because they knew they are supposed to fear God. Are you afraid that this might not be part of my job and that I am going all out at this for real? Well, it may be true, who knows? Am I God? I'm God.

SIMMON: You ain't shit.
GERMAN: What?
SIMMON: You hear me? You ain't shit.

GERMAN: That's why I don't want to be your friend.

SIMMON: Fuck you, then.

GERMAN: You too. Sticks and stones may break my bones, but words will never hurt me.

SIMMON: You, God? Shit, you ain't even a man yet. Bet you don't even have hair in your ass.

GERMAN: I have hair all over me: on my balls, on my chest, on my legs, on my arms.

SIMMON: Peach fuzz on your face . . .

GERMAN: I got hair in my ass, you wanna see?

SIMMON: Yeah.

GERMAN: Here, look. Do I got hair in my ass?

SIMMON: Yep, you have hair in your ass.

GERMAN: See, you don't know nothing.

SIMMON: Never said I knew anything, did I?

GERMAN: You didn't need to, because I knew you didn't know nothing . . .

SIMMON: Then, you just taught me something, right?

GERMAN: Well, that's what I'm here for.

SIMMON: Next thing that's gonna come out of your mouth is "I am carrying out my Father's works." And thunder will blast throughout the yard and the inmates will come to the gates of their freedom: the parole board . . .

GERMAN: Not me, I'm from Queens . . . but I was born in the Lower East Side. My parents are from Puerto Rico and my wife is Jewish . . .

SIMMON: Really? Shit. So fucking what? I didn't ask. I thought you be . . .

GERMAN: You thought that I would hide my private life. I live right here . . .

SIMMON: Look, please, I don't really care about you. You didn't want me to be your friend, so don't treat me like if I said that I am your friend. I've been working here a short bit. My wife's father works in the administration.

GERMAN: So what? My wife's father works in security and her brother is a guard too . . . ha . . . take that.

SIMMON: You still on probationary station?

GERMAN: I'll be off it sooner than you were. I bet ya . . .

SIMMON: Are you going to the annual officers' and captains' dance this year? I am, I got tickets.

GERMAN: Of course, I'm going. What do you think?

SIMMON: I don't.

GERMAN: You don't what?

SIMMON: I don't think at all.

GERMAN: Why not?

SIMMON: Because I don't feel like thinking, that's why.

GERMAN: That's a good enough reason.

SIMMON: Any reason is good enough as long as it has reason.

GERMAN: You laid a fart.

SIMMON: Yeah, so what? Don't you fart?

GERMAN: Yeah, I guess so.

SIMMON: Don't you know?

GERMAN: Of course, I know. They smell.

SIMMON: Have you ever been in the company of a young lady and wanted to lay a fart so bad that you let it out so slow and carefully and . . . ah . . .

GERMAN: Yeah, yeah, yeah, that's happenned to me plenty of times. One time I was in a party and I was holding on to this fart real tight . . . so finally I let loose and the motherfucker was so loud they lowered the music thinking that I had something to say. Funny thing was that not only gas came out, but a whole lot watery shit spread all over my leg and ass. Man, I was stinking for days after that.

SIMMON: Man, that's really funny shit.

GERMAN: No, man, it was really stinking shit.

SIMMON: You're a riot.

GERMAN: Yeah, man, I was great in high school shows.

SIMMON: So was I. I mean, not as a comedian like you, but as a dramatist actor.

GERMAN: Really? That's nice. I always wanted to act . . . as a serious actor, you know . . . never got the break because there was never any part that was right for me, 'cause, well, you know why.

SIMMON: Of course. You guys can't speak English, right? Not like Jose Ferrera . . . he was mean in that picture about that sword fighter.

GERMAN: Yeah, but I didn't like him in it.

SIMMON: You got to be kidding.

GERMAN: Yeah, I am.

SIMMON: He was a mousekateer.

GERMAN: Were you ever in the cadets?

SIMMON: Naw, couldn't afford it. My folks . . .

GERMAN: I was in one when I lived in the Lower East Side.

SIMMON: Did you like it?

GERMAN: Yes and no . . .

SIMMON: Oh, you one of those maybe men?

GERMAN: No, I mean no, I am not a maybe man. I say yes when I have to say yes and no when I have to say no. But with this I really liked it and I didn't like it at the same time, you know what I mean? Isn't there things that you do that you don't like doing and yet do them because you kinda like doing it? No? Well, you see, you know what I mean . . . I was in the cadets and we had these really pretty uniforms: black and gold and red stripes . . . and the band would play behind us when we went to parades . . . real nice . . . but for some reason or another, nobody liked me. I was always the last one to be chosen to play on any of the teams: baseball or basketball or the track and field days that we had in the summer. Those were real nice. We used to chase the girls and those that you caught you had the right to take them prisoner and we would all stick our finger up their cunts and then we would all put them in front of the leader's nose and those that smelled the most would get gold brick detail. Man, you know no one ever came back with non-smelling fingers. Those that did, woo, they would work them to death . . . they would have to do everything in the camp. They would yell out "stomachs in-chest out . . . ass out" and he would come down the ranks and touch everyone's ass. Those who didn't have their ass sticking out enough would have to go take a cold shower. Man he was sure tough.

VOICE: Tough? You ain't tough. You ain't nothing. You'll never be nothing. Tough? Shit, you're a powder puff and you want me to marry you. Shit, I wanna marry a man, not a sissy. Your brothers are men. Why can't you be like your brothers? They are men.

GERMAN: Get out of my thoughts. Now!

SIMMON: What's the matter, man?

GERMAN: Tell her . . . she is inside of me again. she won't leave me alone . . . tell her . . .

SIMMON: Get out from inside of him, whoever you are.

GERMAN: She's still saying that I ain't a man, but I am. Get off me, nigger, get off me. You think I need your help? For what? For what?

SIMMON: Man, I felt . . .

GERMAN: Felt? Feelings? What feelings? The only feelings you got come out in a toiletbowl and you wipe them off on the tissues. I don't need your help. You're just like her, thinking I need help. I need nobody, because I am a man. I am a man. I'm more of a man than a man being a man's man. I am God's man. You see? You see the outline of my dick? It's pretty, ain't it? It's got a beautiful shape. How about yours? Does it curve at the top like mine does? Would you like to see it?

SIMMON: No . . . no, thank you. Listen, why don't you put that rifle back, huh? . . . before the brass sees you?

GERMAN: No . . . I like this rifle and I loaded it with real bullets, man. It's not part of the scene, is it? Up here, you like the Thompson because it makes you feel for real. But me, I like the rifle because it's more accurate. You know what I mean?

SIMMON: I know that if you don't out that thing, there's going to be trouble from the people up front.

GERMAN: Let there be, see if I care . . . because you and the rest didn't think I could do this, did you? But I am showing all of you, ain't I right?

SIMMON: Yeah, man, you are showing us all up. Why don't you call up and get all the people out of here? This way we can do the thing ourselves. You know what I mean?

GERMAN: No, . . . they paid to get in, right? They committed crimes against the people.

SIMMON: We all commit crimes against one another, but shooting people down to prove a point ain't proving nothing, except that you're crazy, and then it falls on your people, you know?

GERMAN: What are you talking about? I ain't going to shoot anybody. Do I look like some kind of a nut?

SIMMON: No, man, you don't look like no nut to me.

GERMAN: Yes, I do.

SIMMON: Well, man, if you insist on saying that you look like a nut, that's up to you, man.

GERMAN: That's what I tell them all, it's all up to me.

SIMMON: What's this about a rumor? You said that you really don't pay attention to rumors, but now you never know . . .

GERMAN: When I was in the cadets I never caught a girl at the track and field meetings.

SIMMON: Maybe you wasn't fast enough.

GERMAN: None of the girls would let me catch them. But I could light a fire faster than anybody else in the troupe.

SIMMON: I bet you could. What about this rumor?

GERMAN: One time I was in the cadets locker room changing my uniform and all the guys were around me looking at me . . . my breasts were large and pointy . . . I was coming of age, I guess. That happens to a lot of boys, you know. They kept looking at me at first. I was shy about it, but, then, every one of them would look and ask me if they could touch them, and more and more I liked the attention . . . they crowded around me, all of them. One day we went on an overnight hike and I slept with two guys that were my best friends in the cadets . . . and that night, Rickie asked me if he could suck on them and I was upset that he could ask me something like that, but I said yes, and he sucked on them, man, he really sucked on them real good . . . the leader came in . . . and he flashed in the light . . . he was making bed checks . . . and he saw us . . . and he got real mad . . . and that morning real early he called everybody together and we went for a long trip into the woods and I had to be by the side of the leader. We stopped at this place in the woods and he told the whole group what he saw . . . then he made me strip and he called everyone to pick up their rifles and two of the boys held me down and the rest spanked me with the rifle butts . . . and then he pulled out his dick. He had a real big dick, bigger than anything I ever seen, and he yelled at me, "Your father said that I should do whatever it takes to make a man out of you," and I think the only way you're ever going to be a man is if you know what it means to be a girl . . . and he put it in me real hard, man. All the guys looked at me and smiled like if they all knew they were next. I thought that all my insides were going to burn right out through my stomach . . . and he pushed and pulled and he cursed me. His dick was full of my shit . . . and blood . . . and then I realized that their smiles meant just what I thought. They were all next, every last one of them pushed and pulled in and out my ass like if there was no tomorrow, see. Later on I quit and moved to Queens and I never was able to fuck any of the new boys. I was always late to the happenings all through college.

SIMMON: Wow, that's heavy . . . a real scar for your mind. What about the rumor?

GERMAN: Rumor? What rumor?

SIMMON: You said that you heard a rumor about something.

GERMAN: Oh, yes, the rumor. Well, one of the informers of the institution informed us with this information . . .

SIMMON: Cut the bullshit out, Rosado.

GERMAN: Okay, killjoy, the rumor is that there's going to be a riot today that's going to be the front for an escape by a group of militants.

SIMMON: A riot?

GERMAN: Yes, a riot. Ain't it exciting? Inmates against the administration. Hostages are supposed to be

75

taken. Haven't you noticed? Look out in the yard. All the guards are either black or Latin. All the whites are in a safe place.

SIMMON: I hope they don't come by this tower with that bullshit.

GERMAN: This is the first place the inmates are gonna hit . . . and they have firebombs, so I was told.

SIMMON: I don't believe it.

GERMAN: You keep talking like you know me a long time. You think that I would lie to you about anything?

SIMMON: Look, maybe them people got the right to complain after the way they are treated in here, out there . . . Haven't you any ears? Don't you speak to your Latin brothers in here? They say that your country is controlled by this country.

GERMAN: What are you talking about my country? This is my country. I fought in the war for it and so did my father, and my oldest brother died for it and for what it stands. My parents were born over there, not me. I am an American citizen and I'm proud to be one. This country has never made me so blue that I would want to be red . . . so don't call me a Puerto Rican. I am an American.

VOICE: When you wanna fuck with me, you are a Puerto Rican. If I don't want to do something, it's Puerto this and Rican that . . .

GERMAN: Get out of my thoughts. . . . Get out of my thoughts, bitch. I can't respect you. After I married you I found out that you're a freak. With my people the word respect means more than the love of God . . . because when people respect you, they will stand with you in any fight . . . and that's what counts . . .

VOICE: When your brothers come around, you become a middle class faggot.

76

GERMAN: That's a lie. I ain't no faggot . . . you're a whore. That's why I can't respect you, because you're a whore. If you were a prostitute, I would respect you because then you would be dealing in quality merchandise and not like a whore that deals just from between her legs. Whore, that's what she is, a no good, low life, back-streeting whore . . . ha ha . . . and you, you are an American too.

SIMMON: I'm the average colored nowhere man.

GERMAN: What is that supposed to mean?

SIMMON: That means that I am a negro . . . with a black man's consciousness in a white man's image of a colored man.

GERMAN: That means that you're a nigger.

SIMMON: Better watch your mouth, boy.

GERMAN: I better not watch nothing, nigger. You tell me that you're a colored man thinking black, living white . . . to me that means that you're a jive nigger.

SIMMON: I told you before to shut the fuck up with that nigger shit, didn't I?

GERMAN: Well, why don't you jump at my throat, nigger?

SIMMON: Why don't you put down that rifle?

GERMAN: Why? So that you can kick my ass?

SIMMON: That's right, punk, so that I can put this foot all the way up to the top of your head, punk.

GERMAN: Why don't you try all that big talk now?

SIMMON: Because you got the power.

GERMAN: You see, there is power.

SIMMON: All over this fucking world.

INMATE VOICE: Mr. Johnson . . . Mr. Johnson, what the hell is going on? They're sounding off the yard.

SIMMON: Calm down, brohter, calm down. Now get down on the ground and I'll make sure nothing happens to you. I got power up here . . . I got power.

INMATE VOICE: What about my boys, Mr. Johnson?

GERMAN: What about them, you stupid sucker? Fuck them, save yourself. You're lucky. He's going to give you the protection. He's going to give you . . . fucker.

SIMMON: Shut the fuck up . . . shut the fuck up, Rosado. You hear me? Shut the fuck up. Go get them.

INMATE VOICE: Right on, brother.

GERMAN: Man, you are stupid. Man, are you dumb. He's one of them militants.

SIMMON: You're lying.

GERMAN: Am I? I never lie . . . for what?

SIMMON: Because you're fucking crazy, that's why.

GERMAN: I am not crazy. There is nothing wrong with me.

SIMMON: Shut up. You don't know what you're talking about.

GERMAN: Did you get the information or did I?

SIMMON: So what? That doesn't mean anything.

GERMAN: They got gas bombs. Shit, fucker, that means a lot. You ever see a man burn to death?

SIMMON: Yes, I have.

GERMAN: You scream all the way until you are dead. So now make a decision . . . about death . . . about killing . . . Mr. Average Colored Man in the Middle of the Road.

SIMMON: Shut up. You don't know what you're talking about. I know people.

GERMAN: You know people, you know people.

SIMMON: He's my friend . . . I know him. He's an inmate, but he's my friend.

78

GERMAN: Yeah, but you don't know yourself . . . you think you do, you think you know yourself, but you don't, fucker. You don't know shit. I told that to you the minute I saw you. He's your friend, heh? What if, for all this time, he had been planning on this break and was just playing friendly to get close to you, to carry this out, to carry this escape? You fool, you fucking fool, we're gonna be burnt alive.

SIMMON: You're not worried about it.

GERMAN: Because I want to die . . . but I want to watch you squirm as you go through this whole shit . . . he catching you unaware . . . yeah, you know people . . . you know people so well that you put yourself in a position to die. A fucked up death at that, ain't it? But like I said, you are God. What you're going to do, it's your creation. God, make it great. Are you going to shoot to kill? Are you going to shoot to wound? Are you going to let them get away? What are you going to do? One firebomb up here and we're through. And I found my out. What a plot for a movie. I should have been a movie script writer. What a plot . . . taan-tannramm. Supernigger makes his move. Here come your friends and they are coming running like the devil. It looks like they ain't going to stop at the fence.

INMATE VOICE: Mr. Johnson they're beating everybody. I'm coming over the tower.

SIMMON: That's off limits.

INMATE VOICE: They're killing me, Mr. Johnson. Don't shoot.

German is laughing. Simmons takes the rifle from him.

LIGHTS

79

Irving

Irving

The People in the Play:

IRVING HOROWITZ: A closet gay, Jewish.
MIMI: Irving's sister, late teens, early twenties, hip.
BUTCH: Black and bisexual.
RICHARD: Irving's younger brother, cool and preco-
*   cious.*
DAD: Irving's very straight father.
MOM: Irving's very straight mother.
AL KOOPERMAN: Mom's brother, a garment tycoon who
*   puts money ahead of family.*

IRVING: Ah, gee, Uncle Al, ah, please Uncle Al . . .
come on, Uncle Al, but Uncle Al . . . it's important, Uncle Al . . . that's not a fair question, Uncle Al . . . no, I didn't mean that you're unfair,
Uncle Al, just that it's an unfair question, Uncle
Al, no, Uncle, I really mean it that I don't mean
it. I really mean it, Uncle Al, I really do, Uncle
Al, Uncle Al, just 'cause I say that you ask an
unfair question doesn't mean that I really think
you're an unfair man, just that you ask an unfair
question, Uncle Al. It simply means, Uncle Al,
that you ask an unfair question. That's all and it
doesn't mean that you're an unfair man, Uncle Al.
No, Uncle Al . . . but . . . but . . . yes, Uncle
Al . . . you're right, Uncle Al. Uncle Al, you are
the fairest of men . . . yes, Uncle Al, you are also
the fairest man in the garment district, I mean,
business . . . Uncle Al, listen to me . . . Uncle
Al, can't you take an hour or two out of your tax
return forms to come up here with me, it's really
important . . . no, Uncle Al, nothing is as important as tax returns . . . No, Uncle Al, I don't think
you should cheat the government. No, Uncle Al,
you should not neglect the family business. Yes,
Uncle Al, I wanna have a summer job every summer that I'm out of work . . . Uncle Al, I am part
of the family, right? Right! So I guess that means
you will not show up at the gathering. No, Uncle
Al, what I want to announce is not routine. No,
Uncle Al, my announcement is not about me join-
ing the marines . . . no, Uncle Al, I am not con-
verting into any other religion . . . no gurus,
Uncle Al . . . it's not the Navy. No, Uncle Al,
listen to me, it's nothing as drastic as soldiering
for anyone at any time, anywhere on this planet.

No, Uncle Al, I am not getting married to a sch-
wartza or a schickza . . . Uncle Al, will you listen
to me? No, Uncle Al, I am not going back to
school . . . I had enough of school . . . the Peace
Corps? . . . I'm not that crazy . . . No, Uncle Al,
I did not become a member of the Jewish Defense
League . . . No, I am not going to Israel to no
kibutz . . . look, Uncle Al, are you going to come
over or not? No, I am not threatening you, Uncle
Al . . . I have respect, Uncle Al . . . I apologize,
Uncle Al . . . yes, Uncle Al, we will speak on it
tonight . . . thank you, Uncle Al.

*He hangs up, gives the finger to the phone, mimics his uncle
asking questions . . . phone rings.*

IRVING: Hello . . . oh, it's you . . . listen, I have no
time today for an obscene call . . . fuck you,
too . . . no, listen don't do that. Look, if you're
gonna jump off the bridge, jump, dammit, and
stop bothering me today. If you don't mind, I
would like to hang up and finish preparing the
house for my family . . . yes, I have a mother . . .
yes, I love her very much . . . no, I never wanted
to . . . hey, what is this? Who are you, Sig Freud?
Oh, I see, you go to an analyst. Okay, if that's
what turns you on . . . fuck you . . . oh, sure,
anything . . . any time, except real late . . . I'm a
theatre person . . . Hey, by the way, I'm gay . . .
hello, hello, aw shit, he hung up on me . . . you
can't even depend on these crank callers . . .

Door bell rings.

MIMI: Hello, sucker.

85

IRVING: Hi, sap.

MIMI: This is Butcher . . . Butcher this is my baby brother, Irving.

BUTCH: Hi, call me Butch.

IRVING: Hi, Butch . . .

MIMI: What you got to drink?

BUTCH: What you got for the head?

IRVING: A hat.

MIMI: My baby brother still tells corny jokes, Butch.

IRVING: I wish that you would please stop referring to me as your baby brother . . .

BUTCH: You smoke?

IRVING: No, it's supposed to be hazardous to your health

MIMI: He means grass, dummy.

IRVING: Once in a while.

BUTCH: Is this one of those whiles?

IRVING: With my mom and dad on the way here, hardly . . .

BUTCH: You mind if I light up a joint?

MIMI: No.

IRVING: Yes.

BUTCH: Well, which is it, yes or no?

IRVING: This is my house and I say no.

MIMI: Irving!

IRVING: Okay, go in the bedroom and take a can of air spray with you, just in case, you know what I mean?

BUTCH: No, I don't.

MIMI: What is this all about, anyway, Ira?

IRVING: Please stop calling me Ira . . . and you'll find out what this is all about soon enough, big sister . . . in due time.

BUTCH: *(From the bedroom.)* You've done time?

IRVING: No.

BUTCH: Oh, I thought you said something about time.

IRVING: I did . . .
BUTCH: Then you did serve time.
IRVING: Only in my mother's womb.
BUTCH: In the tombs . . . yeah, that's a heavy place . . .
IRVING: Yeah, it sure is . . .
BUTCH: What did you say, brother man?
IRVING: I said that me and my sister are discussing per-
           sonal family problems and I would appreciate it if
           you kept out of it.
BUTCH: What makes you think I wanna be in your fam-
           ily, anyway, especially have you being ashamed of
           having done time.
MIMI: What would you like to drink, butcherman?
IRVING: You name it.
BUTCH: You got any pluck?
IRVING: Any what?
MIMI: Wine.
IRVING: Yeah, but it's non-union grape wine.
MIMI: How would you have something like that in your
           house?
IRVING: Because it's my house.
MIMI: But, Irving, don't you know anything about the
           struggle these people are going through, trying to
           unionize the workers of the fields, my God!
IRVING: Don't you use the Lord's name in vain and, be-
           sides, it's the cheapest wine I could get. You know
           I'm not exactly making all the money in the world.
MIMI: So you sell out the movement for a bottle of cheap
           wine.
BUTCH: Your brother sure plays himself cheap.
IRVING: Look, the only movement I'm interested in is
           the dance class.
BUTCH: Of course, I got class. I'm with her, ain't I?
IRVING: Look, would you please mind your business.
BUTCH: (Coming out the bedroom.) Look here, buddy,

unless you can fight, you better dig yourself, with the way you come out your mouth, 'cause the way I witness things with you is that you're too light to fight and too thin to win.

IRVING: Poetry!

MIMI: So are his oversized fists.

IRVING: I better warn you, Mr. Butcher, that I happen to hold a brown belt in the deadly art of karate.

BUTCH: And I think I better warn you that I hold an oversized razor . . .

MIMI: Will you two please stop it, already, you make me feel uneasy . . .

IRVING: Not enough sun and vitamins . . .

BUTCH: Well, I don't know about the vitamins, but I tell you one thing, she gets enough of the sun . . .

MIMI: Funny.

IRVING: Very . . . a regular slappy white.

MIMI: So, who's coming over?

IRVING: I just finished talking Uncle Al into appearing . . .

MIMI: Really . . . you got him away from the tax forms.

BUTCH: He's like my Uncle Wilbur, aways making out the numbers . . .

IRVING: It's not the same thing, taxes and what your Uncle Wilbur does.

BUTCH: Sure, it's the same thing.

IRVING: How do you figure that?

BUTCH: Well, look at it this way: taxes deal with numbers and bread, right? Well, so does the numbers . . . numbers deal with numbers and bread too . . .

IRVING: You figured that out all by yourself, didn't you? . . .

MIMI: What's your sign, Butch?

BUTCH: Gemini.

IRVING: I'm a saggetteri.
MIMI: Great combination you two make.
IRVING: You two make a great combination, too . . .
MIMI: Thank you, Irving.
IRVING: You probably deserve each other . . .
BUTCH: Are you being nasty or what?
IRVING: What.
BUTCH: What?
MIMI: What?
IRVING: He asked me if I was being nasty or what . . . well I'm not being nasty, so I must be being what . . .
MIMI: Whatever you're being, you shouldn't be being it.
BUTCH: That goes for me too . . . whatever you're being, you should be cool.
IRVING: I was just getting warm . . . *(The door bell rings.)*
BUTCH: How long you been in the city?
IRVING: All my life. I was born in Brooklyn.
BUTCH: I'm talking about the city, not the suburbs . . .
MIMI: Who is it, Irving?
IRVING: It's the delivery boy from the Chinese deli.
MIMI: Chinese deli??
BUTCH: Sure, why not, they have Puerto Rican soul food, don't they?
IRVING: Sure, it's been blessed by the neighborhood rabbi. They make some good things to knosh on . . .
MIMI: I thought you told me you were going to have a nice little family party with plenty of food.
IRVING: Well, I lied . . . and besides, you're getting too fat . . . and I don't have the money to spend . . .
MIMI: Can it, will you?
BUTCH: Jesus Christ, cold cuts . . .
IRVING: Would you like some hot cornbread?

MIMI: Irving, how dare you . . .

IRVING: How dare me what? You goddamn liberal broads . . .

BUTCH: Be cool, Irving . . . I can dig where you're coming from, my man . . .

IRVING: Can you?

MIMI: Butch, let me have one of those joints . . .

IRVING: Which you most likely paid for.

MIMI: Irving, you're getting out of hand.

BUTCH: No he ain't, he's on it. You want the roach clip?

MIMI: No thank you, honey.

IRVING: (Stage whispering.) What's all this crap about too thin to win, too light to fight all about?

BUTCH: Well, it's true . . . push comes to shove . . .

IRVING: Well, I'm pushing . . .

BUTCH: And I'm gonna shove . . . Miss Thing . . .

IRVING: And don't call me Miss Thing . . . Mrs. Thing.

BUTCH: Be cool with that shit, Irving . . . you don't want your sister to know where your head is now, do you?

IRVING: Oh, do I have a surprise for you, darling honey.

MIMI: Oh, I forgot the airspray.

BUTCH: Well, Irving, you think the Knicks will take it?

IRVING: Oh, sure, if they change into their lavender gym trunks.

BUTCH: What is it with you, man?

IRVING: What is it with you . . . all I did was answer your question.

BUTCH: I don't think I'm gonna like this party . . .

IRVING: As your people say, it'll all come out in the wash.

BUTCH: Irving, no, this is not what I think that it is, is it?

IRVING: And what do you think this is . . . Butchy Baby?

BUTCH: A coming out party.
MIMI: What kind of party did you say, Butch?
BUTCH: A blowing out party.
IRVING: How about a blow down party?
BUTCH: Come, stop talking loud, will ya?
IRVING: Is there something you don't wish my sister to
           hear?
BUTCH: There sure is . . .
MIMI: Did you call me, loverman?
BUTCH: No, baby, go back into the bedroom.
IRVING: Yes go finish your joint, I think you're gonna
           need your head together pretty soon.
MIMI: My head is together, isn't it, baby?
BUTCH: It sure is, mama . . .
IRVING: It sure is, mama . . . wow, what a lot of crap
           you run out of your face.
BUTCH: Gotta make a living, don't I?
IRVING: Do you have to do it this way?
BUTCH: No, but can you give me an easier way?
IRVING: There are no easy ways to make a living.
BUTCH: Like hell, there isn't . . .
MIMI: What are you two whispering about?
BUTCH: Nothing . . . nothing at all, baby doll.
MIMI: Let me have the roach clip, sugar?
BUTCH: Sure, sweet thing, here . . . me and your
           brother are discussing my relationship with you
           and my intentions.
IRVING: And I must say they're quite honorable.
MIMI: My, Irving, I never thought you'd ask things like
           that.
BUTCH: He is your brother, isn't he? . . . he's con-
           cerned.
IRVING: Yes, I am in more ways than one.
MIMI: My, Irving, that touches me deeply.
BUTCH: Better leave us men alone for a while. Go and
           finish your smoke, baby.

MIMI: Right . . .

BUTCH: Good girl, that sister of yours.

IRVING: And she makes good money and has a little store up some place, as if you didn't know.

BUTCH: I didn't know that at all, and that's scouts honor.

IRVING: You probably stole your scout badge.

BUTCH: So happens I did.

IRVING: How long has this been going on?

BUTCH: What are you talking about?

IRVING: You and my sister?

BUTCH: About two months.

IRVING: You been going out with me for nearly three months.

BUTCH: Just trying to share myself with your family.

IRVING: Fuck you.

MIMI: Listen, this talk has got to end, 'cause the joint's finished and I am not going to spend my time back there waiting. From now until doomsday, until you two decide that I can have a man. I make my own decisions, thank you, Irving . . . and you too Butch!

IRVING: Do Mom and Dad know about you and . . .

MIMI: . . . and Butch, no! I see no reason for them to know any of my personal life, sexual or otherwise, do you?

IRVING: I'm a man.

BUTCH: Really?

MIMI: Yeah! What is that supposed to mean . . . that I lie down and wash dishes?

IRVING: Not a bad idea, if only you knew how to cook.

BUTCH: Restaurants are good enough for me.

IRVING: So are fried roaches . . . and boiled rats . . .

MIMI: You want another drink, Butch?

BUTCH: Yeah, honeychild.

IRVING: I would like one.

MIMI: Get your own. *(Doorbell rings.)*
IRVING: I'll get it.
BUTCH: What makes you think anybody else was . . . ?

Telephone rings.

MIMI: You want me to answer it, Irving?
IRVING: Yeah, go ahead . . . if it's any of my friends,
           I'm not home.
BUTCH: I didn't know you had friends.
IRVING: They come in all colors too . . . Mom . . .
           Dad . . . Richard.
MOM: Irving, my little baby!
DAD: How are ya, Irving?
RICHARD: Hey, Irv . . . qué pasa . . . it's Spanish for
           what's happening!
IRVING: Hey! Where'd you get them clothes, Richard?
RICHARD: They call me Rickie on the Lower East Side.
MOM: He moved out of the house. He thinks he's a man,
           already.
RICHARD: Hey, mom! But I am!
DAD: Then he moves all the way down there with all
           those Porto Ricans and . . .
RICHARD: Hey! What's happening, my man?
DAD: Who's this, a friend of yours, Irving?
MOM: Hello, Mimi. Mimi, what's the matter with you?
           Look, she's white!
BUTCH: Well, she's not exactly in my complexion
           league.
DAD: Mimi . . . Mimi . . .
MIMI: *(Screams.)* There's a nut on the phone, Daddy.
IRVING: Oh, my God . . . give me the phone. He's not a
           nut . . .
MIMI: What do you mean, he's not a nut. I pick up the
           phone like any normal . . .

MOM: . . . good Jewish girl . . .

MIMI: . . . and there's this breathing and nasty words and suggestion . . . God almighty, what is this world coming to?!

IRVING: Will you shut up, already. He's listening.

DAD: He should listen to what I'm going to say to him.

RICHARD: Be cool, Dad . . .

DAD: Do I look like a refrigerator to you?

RICHARD: Come on, Dad.

IRVING: Come on, Dad. He's a friend of mine.

MOM: A friend of yours?

IRVING: Well, not exactly a close friend . . . no, we're not friends, don't worry about it . . . but I told you I had company coming to my house today . . . no, no, don't jump off the bridge . . . it's too cold out tonight . . .

BUTCH: Tell him the water is polluted too. He'll get sick!

DAD: What about my daughter? She is sick.

RICHARD: Aw, come on, Dad, there's nothing wrong with Mimi.

MIMI: Like hell, there isn't . . . how would you like to pick up the phone and hear someone breathing on the other side?!

RICHARD: I think it'll be a very hip thing if it happens to me. Most of the time I do it to other people.

MOM: Richard!!

RICHARD: Rickie, Mom! Rickie . . . that's my new name.

DAD: Rickie Harris . . . he's ashamed of Horowitz . . . how could anyone be ashamed of their family name?

BUTCH: I don't know, my name is Castleton . . . Butcher Castleton.

MOM: Butcher??

94

DAD: It's a name, Mother.

IRVING: I mean, like Mimi, how could you call the caller?

BUTCH: The who?

IRVING: I don't know his name, so I call him the caller.

MIMI: You got some friends, I must say.

RICHARD: Everybody needs friends.

MIMI: But do they need freaks for friends?

MOM: Miriam, don't speak like that.

DAD: That's your daughter . . .

MOM: Now she's my daughter . . .

RICHARD: I admit that she's my sister.

MIMI: Thank you, Richard.

RICHARD: Think nothing of it, Sis.

IRVING: . . . Because it's nothing.

MIMI: Screw you.

MOM: Miriam!

DAD: Miriam!

RICHARD: Go on, Sis, . . . with the bad mouth.

MOM: Where do you pick up such language?

IRVING: Most likely from her boyfriend.

DAD: Well, I sure'd like to meet this boyfriend of hers.

MOM: So would I . . . I have one or two things to say to him.

IRVING: You already met him . . . Dad . . . Mom . . . Richard . . . meet Mimi's male friend.

BUTCH: Hi, folks . . . the name is Butcher Garvey Castleton, my friends call me Butch and my foes call me motherfucker.

RICHARD: Can I call you Butch?

BUTCH: You can call me as you please, it's your world, my man. I'm just visiting . . .

RICHARD: Vaya . . . that's Spanish.

BUTCH: It's Puerto Rican for anything that's good . . .

MOM: Are you planning anything serious?

DAD: Are you planning anything serious?

MIMI: Mom already asked that question, Daddy.

DAD: So she did . . .

IRVING: Would anybody like a drink?

MOM: What's the strongest thing you have, son?

IRVING: Scotch.

MOM: Make it a double.

DAD: Mother . . .

MIMI: Mother . . .

RICHARD: Mother . . .

BUTCH: *(Dad chugs his drink down.)* Wow, you do better than my dad.

RICHARD: Hey, man, are you a Panther?

MOM: Make it a triple.

DAD: That goes for me too.

BUTCH: No, my man, I'm a pussy cat.

MIMI: Mother, I am not getting married to Butch.

MOM: You're not?

DAD: You're not?

RICHARD: You making it common law?

DAD: Richard, keep your ideas to yourself.

MIMI: No, Mom, we're just friends.

IRVING: Intimate special friends . . .

DAD: Oh . . .

MIMI: Why are you both acting so hysterical about my relationship with Butch? . . . you taught me to be independent of others . . . to make my own decisions . . .

DAD: Maybe we teach you too much too soon.

BUTCH: What is that supposed to mean?

DAD: Nothing important.

IRVING: Everything you've always said has been important. All of a sudden it's not . . . strange happennings going on here, Dad.

MIMI: In more ways than one, my darling Irving . . .

96

BUTCH: Are you apprehensive of the relationship between your daughter and me because I am a black
man?

DAD: It has nothing to do with the color of your skin,
young man.

MOM: None whatsoever.

RICHARD: Boy, are you crazy . . . I don't mean "boy"
in the manner that it has been meant to be for your
people over the years . . .

IRVING: Oh, shut up already with your I'm-a-hip-Jew
routine, Richard. It's getting down right boring.

RICHARD: I'm just a human being trying to make con-
tact with other human beings, big brother.

IRVING: Why don't you write your letters to the *New
York Times* and keep them in your coldwater flat?

RICHARD: Out of the closet, into the street, Irving . . .

MOM: Get what out of the closet?

MIMI: So, Richard, you had the same feeling about Irving?

DAD: What feeling are you talking about?

MOM: Mr. Butch, it has nothing to do with the color of
your skin.

MIMI: No, then why are you so up tight?

RICHARD: They're not up tight . . .

MIMI: Like hell, they ain't!

DAD: You're already beginning to sound like one of
them.

MIMI: Like one of what?

MOM: Like one of them non-Jewish friends of Richard.

DAD: So, you see, Mr. Butch, it has nothing to do with
your being black at all.

RICHARD: None whatsoever.

MOM: No, only that you're not Jewish.

BUTCH: According to Jewish law, if I'm not mistaken,
your grandchildren will be Jewish and will fall under Jewish law.

MOM: My grandchildren! Oh my, oh my . . . my heart! . . .

DAD: Quick, get her purse.

MIMI: What's wrong, Mom?

MOM: My heart . . . oh, my heart . . . I'm dying . . . my heart . . .

BUTCH: Jesus H. fucking Christ!

RICHARD: Here, Dad, her purse.

DAD: Get the pills, you dumb ox.

MOM: Everything is turning black . . . I hear the Lord calling me.

IRVING: Aw, come on, Mom, he don't even know your name.

DAD: Irving, I can't believe it.

IRVING: Look, she's always catching heart attacks.

MIMI: It could be the real thing this time.

IRVING: You sound like something out of "Ben Casey."

RICHARD: And you sound like someone out of Hitler's youth.

IRVING: *(Striking Richard.)* Son of a bitch!

MIMI: Stop it, you two, . . . stop it . . . Mom is choking on a heart attack and you two are battling each other . . . this is ridiculous . . .

RICHARD: You fight just like one too.

MIMI: Like one what?

IRVING: Why don't you two go ahead and broadcast it to the world . . .

DAD: How are you, Mother?

MOM: I'm alright, just give me some brandy . . .

DAD: You have any brandy, Irving?

IRVING: Right there on the table, Dad.

DAD: how can you two fight over whatever you're fighting over when your Mother is dying of a heart attack?

MOM: What is going to happen to us when we retire to the home for the aged?

BUTCH: We don't send our old to them places . . .
RICHARD: That's family love.
BUTCH: Also not being able to afford it . . . (*Door bell.*)
MIMI: I'll get it.
AL: Okay, where is that boy? Hello, Mimi.
MIMI: Hello, Uncle Al.
AL: Oh, I see you still consider me your uncle . . .
RICHARD: Hello, Uncle Al.
AL: Well, if it isn't the longhair freedom of expression, cosmic traveling, neo-wandering Jew of the new world!
BUTCH: Shitttt!
MIMI: This is Butch, my friend.
AL: Your chauffer, you said? . . .
BUTCH: He man, my man . . .
MOM: Oh, my heart.
DAD: Calm down, Mother.
AL: You have another heart attack, again Ruth?
MOM: I almost didn't make it this time, Al.
AL: I'll bet.
DAD: Hello, Al.
AL: Hello, Abe.
DAD: Long time no see.
AL: Long time since you took the company and most of the business with you, Abe.
MOM: Let's not start with personal family problems.
AL: Why not, we're in front of the family?
DAD: Not the whole family.
BUTCH: You got a nigger in the woodpiles . . .
AL: Let me have a drink.
IRVING: What's that, Uncle Al?
AL: My taxes.
IRVING: But, Uncle Al, this is supposed to be a party for an important announcement . . .
AL: I don't have to look at you to hear you make a speech. (*Phone rings.*) I got it.

MIMI: No.

IRVING: No.

AL: There's somebody named Ramon . . . says he got "Panama Red."

MOM: Panama is red? Since when? I thought Cuba was the only communist Latin country.

DAD: So is Chile.

RICHARD: Panama red has nothing to do with politics, Mom.

BUTCH: You can say that again, buddy.

MIMI: Irving . . . Irving . . . shame . . . shame . . . Panama red!

AL: Well, what ya want to tell the man . . . time is money, you know.

IRVING: I'll speak to him. Hello, Ramon . . . how are you? No, that was my uncle Al . . . no, no hassles . . . give me one . . . no, tomorrow evening . . . adiós.

BUTCH: Necessity . . .

IRVING: Excuse me, what did you say?

BUTCH: All I said was necessity.

IRVING: What about necessity?

BUTCH: Adiós . . . dame una bolsa de yerba . . .

AL: You want a bag of grass?

IRVING: Uncle Al speaks very good Spanish.

AL: You have to, it's a necessity . . . when you got a bunch of Puerto Ricans working for you that just jumped off the boat . . . excuse me, airplane nowadays . . . and they can't speak a word of English . . . you'd be surprised how many of them can speak Yiddish before they can speak English.

BUTCH: That's what I was saying, my man.

AL: I am not your man . . . I am my own man, have been, will be until the Lord comes to visit me and then I'll give him an argument about it too.

100

BUTCH: Hallelujah, praise the Lord!

Shots are heard.

IRVING: I recommend that everyone stay away from the
           window.
MIMI: Why?
BUTCH: That was no backfiring that you heard, baby.
MOM: Oh, dear God.

More gunfiring.

DAD: Why don't we all sit on the floor?
RICHARD: Not a bad idea.
AL: Well, I am one that does not believe that it's a good
           idea.
IRVING: Uncle Al!
BUTCH: That's up to you, my man, but where I come
           from, when you hear shots, you duck and pray the
           cop isn't aiming in your direction . . .
RICHARD: Well, I'm with Uncle Al.
AL: If we don't bow to God . . . I definitely am not bow-
           ing to man or his creations of death.
RICHARD: Me neither.
IRVING: Then why don't you stop making believe that
           you're tying your shoes . . .
RICHARD: There.

Police siren.

BUTCH: The man.
IRVING: Ditch the shit.
RICHARD: *(Laughing.)* Did you see him go for his
           pocket.
DAD: Officer! *(By window.)* Officer, there's one over

there, Officer . . . hello, up here, officer!

IRVING: Dad, what the hell are you doing?

BUTCH: Your old man is a rat.

MOM: Dad, mind your business.

IRVING: Dad, you wanna get me burnt out of here?

DAD: What are you talking about? I'm just trying to help the police.

BUTCH: Ain't this a bitch?

RICHARD: In this neighborhood that's a no-no, Dad, 'cause the guy could have taken a shot at you.

MOM: God . . .

DAD: That's why I tried to warn the officer.

RICHARD: Not the man on the run, Dad, but the cop.

BUTCH: That's right, Mr. Horowitz, when they're after somebody who has a gun, they're as jumpy as a dope fiend with his jones coming down . . .

DAD: Though He may slay me, yet I will trust in Him and I will serve Him without hope of reward.

BUTCH: That's pure unadulterated bullshit.

AL: Watch your language, young man . . .

IRVING: Poor education.

MIMI: Crap.

MOM: Watch your language, young lady.

RICHARD: Young Lady?? *(Giggles.)* Mom, you better watch out.

MIMI: Up yours.

AL: Well?

IRVING: Well what?

AL: Well, what did you invite me up here for?

DAD: You mean you have to have something special to come and visit your nephew?

AL: You mean you have to take all the business to be rid of your troubles?

DAD: What are you talking about?

AL: Don't hand me this innocent mashugana talk.

RICHARD: You two are still fighting over the split?

AL: If it had been a split, I wouldn't be fighting and I'll let you know, young man, that we are not fighting, at least I am not fighting with anybody . . . I am just bringing up facts about a certain backstabbing-false-teeth-balding-type-wearing-a-hole-in-the-wall rat that married my sister on the run . . .

DAD: Ten years, Al . . . ten years, Al, that I put up with your ignorances . . . your stupidity . . . your . . . your . . . hard headed stubbornness . . . your . . .

MOM: Your blood pressure . . . don't get exited! . . .

AL: Let him get excited, maybe he'll pop a blood vessel.

BUTCH: And ruin little Irving's rug.

AL: Ten years of your soft bleeding heart for every crook that ever took a dress off a rack.

DAD: Listen to him talk . . . the strong gut Sampson of the garment district . . .

MOM: Your blood rpessure, dear!

DAD: Blood pressure . . . blood pressure . . .

AL: Yeah, stay out of this . . .

DAD: This is my blood pressure, this nut brother of yours!

AL: Who are you calling a nut?

DAD: You and your whole family are crazy and lazy, with no imagination whatsoever to foresee the smell of horseshit in a stable. You think . . . you think . . .

IRVING: Dad, are you all right?

MIMI: Dad . . . Dad . . . please, calm down.

DAD: Calm down?

RICHARD: Yeah, Dad, be cool before you blow a fuse.

AL: Well, at least he comes out with the truth of how he feels about us . . .

BUTCH: I think I better leave . . . strangers are not, well . . .

AL: Be quiet, young man.

MIMI: You're my guest.

RICHARD: My man, right on.

IRVING: My man, limp wrist.

DAD: You stay, the whole world should know this . . .

AL: The whole world, no less.

DAD: The whole world should know how narrow minded
you think.

AL: My thinking can't be that narrow if you feel the
whole world should be informed about my
thoughts.

DAD: That's all you were: a lot of empty words, for
all the time that we worked together . . . for all
the times that we traveled together . . . for all the
times that we ate together and you stuck me with
the bill . . . that's what you are, Al, an empty dic-
tionary sticker. What time did you ever take the
blame for any business failures? Not one time did
you ever take on the responsibilities for being
wrong. It was always "good old reliable Abe" that
took the blame . . . but when something good
came along, it was "industrious Al" who got the
credit . . . I helped build that company from the
ground up too, Al . . .

AL: I never said different . . .

DAD: No, you never said different . . . but also you
never said anything that would make the rest of the
workers proud of me . . . I was the cutter, Al.

AL: I was the business head, Abe.

DAD: But so was I . . . every holiday . . . there was an
office party, you always had someone introduce
you . . . "Ladies and gentlemen" . . . "fellow
workers" . . . and on and on it went until a half
hour later . . ." and here is the man who gave us
all an avenue to exist in this world of bill collec-
tors: Al Kooperman" . . . then you would go

and make a speech of your headaches, of your end-
less quest to keep them all employed, enabling
them to feed and clothe their families . . . what a
lot of crap those office parties were, and why was
it that it was you that would introduce me "here's
my partner, Abe Horowitz" . . . I barely ever
heard my name . . . and this year-after-year pat-
tern never changed . . . the employees did, so he
always used the same speech every year, with the
same introduction . . . that was written by Mr. Al
Kooperman himself . . .

AL: So that's it!

DAD: No, that's not it . . .

RICHARD: What is it, Dad?

MOM: Be quiet, Richard.

DAD: No, that's not it, but why didn't you ever have a
speech like that for me? Why didn't you ever have
an introduction like that for me?

AL: Why didn't you have it for yourself? I wrote my own
introduction and I wrote my own speeches.

DAD: Speeches?!

AL: Well, all right, a speech, but that doesn't alter the
fact that I did write it myself . . . and had the guts
to read it over and over again . . . I always thought
you weren't interested in that kind of attention.

DAD: Well, I was.

BUTCH: Can I have another glass of wine, please.

IRVING: Dinner is . . .

AL: I'm not hungry.

DAD: Neither am I.

MOM: Frankly, son, I couldn't eat very much myself.

RICHARD: This is more appetizing than food right now,
Irv.

MIMI: I'm on a diet . . . a piece of bread with butter will
do fine.

IRVING: How about you?
BUTCH: Why not . . . there's nobody else here but you
          and me.

Irving goes to the record player.

IRVING: Music . . .
BUTCH: Soft . . .
IRVING: Lights.
BUTCH: Soft.
IRVING: I have candles . . .
BUTCH: All the better.

*Music: "I'm in the mood for love." The family keeps up the
argument. Irving and Butch set up the table, sit down to eat,
never taking their eyes from each other.*

DAD: But, I fixed you good, didn't I? How is the busi-
          ness coming along?
AL: Great, Abe.
DAD: I worked every day out there on the table with the
          men. Not once did you ever put in an appearance
          until payday.
AL: I worked my way up to be a boss . . . my working
          days are over.
DAD: Were over . . .
AL: You took all the experienced cutters with you.
DAD: You kept all the contracts.
AL: What are contracts without the people to produce
          them? I had lost two of them already, plus the pay-
          ments on the damaged garments.
BUTCH: Did you cook this yourself?
IRVING: Family recipe.
BUTCH: Good.
IRVING: Thank you.

BUTCH: You sure you wanna do what you plan to do?
IRVING: I see no reason why not.
BUTCH: I do.
IRVING: Them? They don't miss me. They don't even miss me in my own home . . . they wouldn't miss me later on . . .
BUTCH: What would you gain?
IRVING: What would I lose?
MOM: And you dear are becoming as big as a zeppelin.
MIMI: If you don't mind, Mom . . .
RICHARD: Go on girl, give her a good one for both of you.
MIMI: Up yours!
IRVING: If I stood up right now and announced to them my feelings . . . my lifestyle . . . they would all leap up in the air with glee . . . and pour wine into my shoes and drink and toast my new found happiness and we would celebrate for days . . . and days and days . . .
BUTCH: Really?
IRVING: No, it's just one of those bullshit dreams sons have in front of their families . . .
BUTCH: Here's to dreams.
IRVING: And may we never wake up.
AL: So, how are the taxes treating you?
DAD: They don't treat me well at all.
AL: How's that?
DAD: Have you ever heard of accountants?
AL: Yeah, sure, they're for people who don't have the guts and brains to cheat the government with their own wits, so they get a front man.
BUTCH: So, you really are going through with it.
IRVING?   Of course, you don't think I brought all these people together just for good old times.
BUTCH: Are you going to say anything about me and? . . .

IRVING: No . . . not unless they ask me if I have a lover.
BUTCH: By the looks of it they won't.
IRVING: Richard . . .
BUTCH: The pseudo hip . . .
IRVING: Yes, the pseudo hip . . . the would-be wise child of Mr. and Mrs. Horowitz is pretty bright.
BUTCH: He must use good toothpaste.
IRVING: My . . . my . . . how dry we get when we fear the truth.
BUTCH: I fear nothing.
IRVING: Except yourself.
BUTCH: Don't go into your guru kick on me, Irv . . .
IRVING: Ohmmmmm.
BUTCH: What I'm basically saying is simply, if you're gonna drag your shit into the street, leave mine alone.
IRVING: It's my coming out party, not yours.
BUTCH: Look, man, why this suddeen rush to let the world know you're what you are? . . . would it make a difference?
IRVING: That's what I hope to find out . . .
BUTCH: And if it did? . . .
IRVING: Well, it does.
BUTCH: Look, man, why not just let your people die in peace?
IRVING: Have they ever let me live in peace?
MOM: What are you saying, Irving?
DAD: I've never gotten into your life, Irving.
RICHARD: Neither have I . . . nor anyone else, for that matter, Irving. In fact, Irving, you remind me of a hermit.
BUTCH: He's hardly that.
MIMI: How would you know?
RICHARD: Why are you rapping that down anyway?
AL: Yeah, Irving, what's it all about?

MOM: I don't understand the meaning of we not letting
         you live in peace.
AL: That makes no sense at all.
IRVING: It makes a great deal of sense when you are
         what I am.
AL: And what the hell is that . . . a rapist . . . a
         killer . . . an undercover rabbi?
IRVING: A homosexual.

SILENCE.

PAUSE.

AL: Yeah, well, go see a psychiatrist.
RICHARD: Are you a member of the Gay Activist Alli-
         ance?
MOM: I don't understand.
IRVING: What's there to understand, Mom? I'm vulnera-
         ble . . . as soft as a water balloon . . . which any-
         one can burst at will . . . for fun . . . for
         spite . . . for abuse . . . for whatever neurotic rea-
         son. See, Mom, anyone can write grafitti about me
         in any public john where a blank space stares at a
         magic marker. Whenever a person goes into a pub-
         lic toilet or any toilet, for that matter, and he has in
         his possession a magic marker, besides relieving
         himself, he has one other purpose for going in
         there: that's either to hurt somebody by writing
         silly things on the walls, such as Irving Horowitz
         is a homosexual, or he's going to advertise him-
         self, his wit, his poetic sense, his disapproval of
         politics today, commentaries on the state of the na-
         tion, on the state of his mind, his desires or his lost
         religion . . . A man with a magic marker is a
         hired killer, like a soldier in Vietnam or a police-

man in the South Bronx. Some use a gun and some use a pen, while others don't give a shit how they use their tongue . . .

MOM: I don't understand . . .

AL: Oy vey ist mir! You mean you got me out here to tell me you're a faggot?

MOM: I don't believe him . . .

RICHARD: I do . . .

DAD: Why didn't you send us all a letter?

AL: Yeah, why the hell you got us all together for? . . . a telegram would have been just as good.

IRVING: Yeah, I could see it now: "Dear Uncle Al—stop—I'm a homosexual—stop—Regards—Irving—"

RICHARD: That's great. You know, I had an experience like that in the army . . . well, actually not me . . . a friend of mine did . . . he did it to get out of the service. Wierd dude . . .

IRVING: You got out early, didn't you, Richard?

RICHARD: Yeah, but for nothing that fucking wierd. I ain't no queer.

BUTCH: A poet has spoken.

MIMI: Please, Butch, keep out.

IRVING: He's in.

RICHARD: How deep?

BUTCH: You had to do it, didn't you, Irving? You couldn't play your own card by yourself. You just had to pull my hole card.

IRVING: Well, Butch, I guess it's a game of cards . . .

MIMI: I don't believe it . . . I can't believe it . . . I refuse to believe it . . .

In background Mom's mumbling, "I can't believe it," and "where did I go wrong?"

RICHARD: You're not leaving any room for Mom's "not-believing" statement.

MOM: You don't look like a homosexual.

DAD: You sure don't, kid.

AL: Go see a psychiatrist, there's still time.

MOM: You don't act like a homosexual.

DAD: You sure don't, kid.

AL: Go see a psychiatrist. I have a friend who knows one . . . and he accepts MasterCharge . . .

MOM: No, he'll blame it on me.

RICHARD: Well, Mom, you are a little overbearing at times.

MIMI: At last, I got a sister.

BUTCH: Mimi, that's not necessary.

MIMI: Since when does a man like you buck up a queer?

BUTCH: Why the fuck . . . excuse the language, Mrs. Horowitz, do you have to call him a queer?

MIMI: What would you call him, a sissy?

RICHARD: How about "lover?"

MIMI: Richard, watch yourself.

IRVING: Well, Butch?

BUTCH: It's as good a term as any.

MIMI: I don't believe it.

AL: You mean to tell me he's a homosexual too?

RICHARD: Black and gay.

DAD: A two-time loser.

MOM: Him too? Lord!

MIMI: You mean you and my brother . . . no, no, that's not so. Look, Butch, who do you prefer, me or him?

MOM: Irving, you don't march? . . .

DAD: And if you do, wear sunglasses.

MIMI: Well, Butch, I'm waiting.

BUTCH: For what?

MIMI: For the answer. Who do you prefer?

IRVING: Well, I know who I prefer.

BUTCH: Shut the fuck up.

MIMI: Oh, I see you both are a regular married couple.

IRVING: Well, I wouldn't say that.

MIMI: No, what would you say?

BUTCH: I'm leaving.

MIMI: Taking the easy way out?

RICHARD: A cop-out artist.

AL: The only question I wanna ask is, Irving, do you think it'll keep you from making money?

IRVING: Yes and no, it all depends on how far the gay liberation goes.

AL: Oh, how I hate politics.

MIMI: I don't give a damn about money or politics. I wanna know about Butch . . .

MOM: I can't believe it.

RICHARD: Go get 'em, Sis . . . stay on the case . . .

BUTCH: A regular Sherlock Holmes.

IRVING: Oh shit! You want some notes, Butchy?

MIMI: Why not call him Mary?

BUTCH: Why not call you motherfucker?

IRVING: Down boy, down.

BUTCH: I think both of you are very charming.

IRVING: Why, thank you, Butch.

BUTCH: Think nothing of it.

IRVING: I don't . . .

RICHARD: That gay talk . . .

IRVING: My, my, you know a lot about gays, don't you?

BUTCH: Probably school research, right, Richard?

AL: Look, seriously . . .

IRVING: What makes you think I am not serious?

AL: Irving, enough of this crap. Now that you made your declaration of being a faggot to the family, what next?

BUTCH: The world . . .

112

MOM: Oh, no . . .

DAD: He's kidding . . . you are kidding? . . . He is kidding, isn't he, Irving?

AL: What was the purpose of this whole public address
crap, anyway? Who the hell cares whether you're
a faggot or not?

IRVING: You do.

AL: All I care about is your wealth . . . health . . . and
wealth . . .

RICHARD: So, Butch, you are the nigger in the wood-
pile?

BUTCH: I guess I am.

MIMI: Well, I have never really been selfish, but I'm
leaving. Coming, Butch?

BUTCH: Later.

MIMI: I'll leave the key in the mailbox. Bye, Mom.

MOM: You're leaving at a time like this, at a time of
crisis?

MIMI: What crisis?

MOM: I don't believe it, so I can't say it.

MIMI: Mom . . . Mom . . .

RICHARD: what do you mean there is no crisis? If Irving
hadn't felt there was a crisis in his lifestyle, Sis, he
would have never called us together. If I remember
correctly, you called me and told me Irving said it
was extremely important that we attend this
dinner . . . in fact, you said "emergency."

MIMI: Yes, but that was because he told me that.

MOM: So there, you see there is a crisis.

RICHARD: Are you contemplating suicide, Irving? It's
not worth it . . . live the life you have accepted for
yourself.

IRVING: There is no crisis, Mimi. And Richard, you
keep those Kung Fu slogans to yourself. I just felt
the need to establish in your minds what I am.

113

MOM: Oh, my poor baby . . .

MIMI: Good night, Mom . . . Dad . . . Richard . . . Butch . . . I'll wait up for you.

AL: Listen, Irving, next time you have something on your mind that is as important as what you brought me out here form, why not do like every neurotic in New York does . . . call a 24 hour "help me" or something like that . . . they have suicide lines . . . drug lines . . . drunk lines . . . so I betcha they have a line where faggots can call.

DAD: Al, let me speak to you about . . . come on, Selma . . . it's been great, Irving . . . so long, Richard . . . get a haircut . . .

AL: Let him keep his hair long . . . at the price of a haircut today . . . let me tell you . . . so long, Irving. *(They exit.)*

MOM: I can't believe it . . .

IRVING: Good night, Mom.

BUTCH: Good night, Mrs. Horowitz.

MOM: You too . . . I can't believe it . . .

They sit in silence drinking.

RICHARD: Well I guess I'll be going.

BUTCH: Keep on going on . . . Later baby.

RICHARD: Good night, Ira.

IRVING: You're a bitch, Richard.

RICHARD: Yeah.

IRVING: I love you.

LIGHTS.

114

Sideshow

Sideshow

People in the Play

HECTOR: *the Man, from 11 to 13 years old, Puerto Rican*

MALO: *the Merchant, 15 to 16 years old, Puerto Rican*

CLEARNOSE HENRY: *13 to 15 years old, glue-sniffer, Puerto Rican*

TUTU: *the Smoke Dealer, 16 to 18 years old, Black*

CHINA: *Tutu's girl, 14 to 16 years old, Puerto Rican*

SUGAR: *Prostitute, 15 to 18 years old, Puerto Rican*

LUCKY: *Pimp, 17 to 18, very handsome, Puerto Rican*

PANCHO Kid: *Hustler, 15 to 17, Puerto Rican*

CISSO: *Apprentice Hustler, 12 to 14, Puerto Rican*

CUSTOMER: *Jibaro, 25 to 30 years old, Puerto Rican*

SUPER: *35 to 40, Black*

The latter two roles should be played by the oldest dude in the cast. The first Voice in the play should be male, and the second Voice should be female and motherly. The dance scene should be contemporary dancing.

HECTOR: Hurry, hurry, step right up and see the baddest show in town for only fifty cents.

MALO: Hi, I'm Malo the merchant. I see anything and everything. Anyone care to buy a watch . . . cheap?

NILSA: Hey, mira, Malo, quieres comprar un television brand new? I just liberated it.

MALO: No.

NILSA: Come on, man . . . my jones is coming down . . . it's brand new . . .

MALO: Brand new! Are you crazy? What you think I am, a sap? Shit, this thing has a broken antenna . . . channel button is missing . . .

NILSA: How much you give me?

MALO: Twenty dollars.

NILSA: Twenty dollars? Man, come on, Malo, don't be like that.

MALO: Man, I ain't gonna make the market scene with you, brother. Twenty dollars, take it or leave it.

NILSA: I'll take it . . . later, Malo.

MALO: Later . . .

TUTU: What's happening, people? I'm Tutu. I deal smoke and I do it for a living . . . and this here is my woman, China. She young girl . . . but she cool . . .

CHINA: I'm China, Tutu's woman. He's a good man. I hold his smoke . . . sometimes I help him make a play or run a game.

MALO: Hey, Tutu, wanna buy a T.V. set . . . brand new? Brotherman, dig this here . . . P-a-n-a-s-o-n-i-c and it's got this new antenna . . . you dig . . . short ones so they ain't all over the place getting in your way and shit like that . . .

TUTU: Okay, Malo, cut the shit short, bro. We need one for the bathroom, anyway.

MALO: Hey man, that's cool. This way you don't miss out on the soap opera when you take a shit.

CHINA: Funny! Why don't you talk that foul fuckin' language somewhere else.

TUTU: Yeah, like, be cool, motherfucker.

MALO: Excuse me, sister . . .

TUTU: What'cha want for it?

MALO: Seventy dollars.

TUTU: Later . . .

CHINA: Vayaaaaaa . . .

MALO: Okay, okay, wait a second . . . thirty-five dollars . . . so, okay?

TUTU: What you think, baby?

CHINA: It's cool with me.

MALO: Vaya. Here.

TUTU: Wait up, bro, I ain't gonna be carrying that shit with me all day. I'm out here to make my money, bro. Look, man, you know where I live at, right? Give it to the super, okay? Tell 'im I'll pick it up tonight. Later.

MALO: Later.

PANCHO KID: My name is Pancho Kid. I been out here hustling for two years. I do it 'cause I like the bread and the feeling. This here is Cisco.

CISCO: I'm Cisco. I'm new around here. I'm supposed to be hustling, but I ain't making much money.

CLEARNOSE HENRY: I'm Clearnose Henry and I sniff glue because it's a together thing.

LUCKY: How do you do? My name is Lucky and I'm a gentleman of leisure.

SUGAR: Hi, I'm Sugar. I'm Lucky's Woman. I'm out here hustling the streets for Lucky, trying to make a living, doing the best I can for my man.

NILSA: Me, my name is Nilsa. I'm a dope fiend. Oh, yeah, and a thief.

HECTOR: Hi, my name is Hector. I'm the Man. Welcome to my world.

CHINA: Tutu, I don't wanna hold the smoke no more.

TUTU: Why?

CHINA: 'Cause I'm getting scared, that's why. And besides, you know, that couple from 'cross the street got busted dealing smoke last night.

TUTU: That's because they weren't as cool as we are, baby. And anyway girl, if we did get busted, you think I'd let you take the weight?

CHINA: No.

TUTU: Okay, then, it's settled. Let's go make some money, 'cause there's plenty of it out here.

PANCHO: Cisco come 'ere.

CISCO: What the fuck you want?

PANCHO: I'm gonna teach you something about the hustle.

CISCO: Like what?

PANCHO: Like if you gonna rip off some of your scores, make sure you keep this in mind. Rip off the old ones, 'cause they don't fight back. Now, the young ones you got to be cool with 'cause some of them niggers may be karate black belts and what not. You dig? Now what you do with a young trick is you give them a rap like you ain't got no place to go . . . and that you hungry and shit like that, and if you have to let a tear fall out of your eyes, then you let a tear fall out of your eyes . . . you get into their confidence . . . look around, check out the windows, the strength of the door . . . and also check out if you can cop an extra set of keys . . . if you cop them, get your boys and rip off the dude for everything he got . . . make sure he don't find out you did it.

CISCO: . . . And if he does?

PANCHO: If he does, make sure your boys are packing when he comes around . . . *(Shouts.)* Hector, bring down the basketball.

HECTOR: Wait up, I'm looking for it.

MALO: Come 'ere, everybody, man, come 'ere. Hey, let's do a play.

CLEARNOSE: I don't want to be in no play.

MALO: If you don't want to do nothin', don't do nothin'.

HECTOR: What kind of play?

MALO: Hold up, let me see . . . oh, yeah, remember the time we got busted, me and Clearnose . . . we got sent to Spofford . . . the time when that little kid got fucked, remember . . . ?

Everybody laughs.

MALO: *(To China.)* You be a social worker and *(To Pancho.)* you be a typist and *(To Nilsa.)* you be a guard.

CHINA: I don't want to be no fuckin' social worker.

MALO: Well, you're gonna be a fuckin' social worker. Now we need the kid that got fucked.

Everybody looks at Clearnose.

MALO: Why don't you play the part of the kid?

CLEARNOSE: No way in the world you gonna get me to play that part.

EVERYBODY: Ah, come on, man, don't be like that.

MALO: Come on, let's do it, it's boring around here.

CLEARNOSE: Naw, man, I don't want to play the kid who gets fucked.
MALO: Man, how long you know me? Do it for me, bro.
CLEARNOSE: No.
MALO: I'll give you a box of tubes.
CLEARNOSE: A box of what?
MALO: A box of glue.
CLEARNOSE: All right, all right.
MALO: I'm director.
EVERYBODY: Ahhhh, it figures, it figures . . .
MALO: *(To Pancho.)* Come on, man.
PANCHO: *(Sitting down on some steps.)* I don't want to be in it, man.
MALO: Come on. *(Grabs his hand.)*

Malo pushes everything out of the way, then puts everything back in the same place.

HECTOR: Malo, Malo, look what I got here, a table for the typewriter.
MALO: Naw, get out of here, that's no good . . . where did you get this from?
HECTOR: Right over there.

Malo puts it back, and picks it up again.

MALO: Hey, look what I got here, a table for the type-writer . . . you put it like this, and you put the typewriter right here . . . then the typist can go tack, tack, tack. *(Makes sounds like typewriter.)*

Clearnose is combing his hair.

HECTOR: Come on, man, come in already . . . you're not on Broadway.

MALO: Come on, come 'ere, hurry up, man.

Clearnose walks in. He attracts attention.

HECTOR: God damn, you's a fine Mother, Clearnose.
MALO: *(Directing Clearnose.)* Go into the social work-
er's office.
CHINA: *(As social worker.)* What's your name?
CLEARNOSE: Clearnose.
CHINA Clearnose what?
CLEARNOSE: Clearnose Henry.
CHINA: Room 106. *(Takes Clearnose to the dorm room
and introduces him around.)* Malo, this is
Clearnose Henry. Hector, this is Clearnose
Henry . . .

*China returns to her office, followed by Hector trying to grab
her ass. Malo, Clearnose and Hector sit on the floor.*

MALO: Is this your first time in here?
CLEARNOSE: Yeah.
MALO: It is? Well, let me tell you what goes on around
here. We eat breakfast at six, lunch at eleven and
dinner at seven. Let's see, what should we do
now?
HECTOR: I got an idea, I got an idea . . .
MALO: What?
HECTOR: Let's show him the psychedelic bathroom.
MALO: Naw, man, I got a better idea . . .
HECTOR: What?
MALO: Let's show him the psychedelic bathroom.
HECTOR: That's what I said, dummy.

*All three get up, Malo and Hector grab Clearnose and try to
take his pants down. The landlord enters.*

LANDLORD: Hey, what are you kids doin' here? Shouldn't you be in bed at 2 o'clock in the morning? *(To Malo.)* Hey, didn't I see you around here before? I told you kids not to hang out around here . . . you're disturbing the peace.

MALO: But sir . . .

LANDLORD: *(Landlord overtakes Malo.)* If I catch you here again, I'm gonna call the cops on you.

The landlord exits, Hector and Malo attack Clearnose again. China rushes in.

CHINA: Hey, what you doin' to that kid? *(She grabs Clearnose.)*

MALO: Oh, I know that kid from the Bronx where I live at.

CHINA: You don't live in the Bronx . . . you live in Staten Island.

MALO: Oh, I mean I go to the Bronx just to go dancin'.

Malo starts dancing. China walks away with Clearnose to the office.

CHINA: What you want?

Hector and Malo listen outside the door.

CLEARNOSE: I want a transfer. I want a transfer. There's a whole bunch of faggots in my dormitory trying to fuck me.

MALO: *(As director.)* You don't say it like that. You be Malo and I'll be Clearnose. This is the way you say it: "I want a transfer, I want a transfer, those kids are trying to fuck me." *(Malo says it in an angry manner.)*

124

CLEARNOSE: (Being Malo.) You don't say it like that,
              you say it like this . . . (Clearnose repeats what
              Malo says.)
MALO: What are you doin'?
CLEARNOSE: You told me to be you!!
MALO: Stupid.
CHINA: Who are the kids, can you recognize them?
CLEARNOSE: The one with the ugly face, and the short
              dumb lookin' one over there.
MALO: There's a door there, stupid.
CHINA: No, you can't have a transfer.
CLEARNOSE: What do you mean I can't have a trans-
              fer?
CHINA: (Shouting.) You can't have a transfer!

Clearnose walks out of the office.

MALO: What you doin', remember there's a door there!

*Clearnose goes back and walks through the door and goes
back to the dorm room.*

MALO: You ain't mad about what happened today? It's
         just that when you got up, we forgot to tell you that
         the floor was just waxed, and you fell and we were
         trying to help you up.
HECTOR: What did they ask you in the social worker's
           office?
CLEARNOSE: Nothin', they just wanted to know more
              information about the robbery.
HECTOR: What robbery?
CLEARNOSE: The robbery that got me here, stupid.
MALO: That's not what I heard. I heard you ratted us
         out.
CLEARNOSE: Who told you that?

125

MALO: A little birdie.

CLEARNOSE: I didn't rat you out.

MALO: *(To Pancho.)* Keep chickie . . . *(Malo throws Clearnose against the wall.)* Yes, you did. Stop lying. *(Malo starts choking him. Clearnose is pushed to the floor. Malo is on top of him, strangling him.)*

CLEARNOSE: Ohhhhh, the pain, the pain . . . agony, agony, agony, agony, agony, etc.

Clearnose rolls around on the floor, holding his throat, groaning. He moves toward China, sits on her lap, starts kissing her.

MALO: What are you doin'? You're supposed to be dying . . .

HECTOR: Why don't you die already?

MALO: You see this fist? You're going to die for real. *(Malo pushes Clearnose to the floor and starts choking him again.)* You ever seen in the movies when someone gets choked . . . they die, right?

CLEARNOSE: Yeah.

MALO: Then die, then . . .

Clearnose groans some more, then dies.

CHINA: Boy-slaughter, boy-slaughter!!

Hector is praying and crying over Clearnose, crossing himself and sobbing.

CHINA: *(To Hector.)* Come 'ere. What did you do to that kid?

MALO: Hey, leave my brother alone, leave my brother alone.

CHINA: Then you take the responsibility.

China takes Malo into her office.

CHINA: Why did you kill that kid?
MALO: What kid? *(Playing with her blouse.)* That's a nice blouse.
CHINA: Forget about the blouse. I asked you a question. Why did you kill that kid?
MALO: I didn't kill nobody . . . *(Still looking at the blouse.)* I like the designs on your blouse. *(Touching her collar and moving down to her breasts. Malo's other hand is in his pocket masturbating.)*
HECTOR: Yo, Clearnose, check this out. Malo's jerking off. *(Both Hector and Clearnose imitate Malo.)*
CLEARNOSE: Oh shit. *(He and Hector start laughing and walk away.)* Hey Malo, there's a customer coming.
CHINA: Com' on, let's play a little longer, man.
MALO: You don't support me, bitch. *(Malo grabs his rack and starts selling clothes.)* Ropa, ropa por vender caro y barato. *(Hector runs through the middle of the rack.)* What the hell you doin'? *(Starts chasing Hector, grabs him and takes him to the rack.)* Hey, what the fuck you doin'? This is my motherfuckin' rack. Don't play that shit with me! *(Malo kicks him in the ass.)*

Hector walks over to Clearnose. Clearnose calls him "stupid." Then a customer walks in.

SUGAR: Hey, Mister,you wanna have a nice time?
CUSTOMER: No, no, I don't got no money. You take credit? Food stamps?
SUGAR: Hey, pendejo!

127

TUTU: *(Calls customer over.)* You wanna buy some smoke.

CUSTOMER: You want a cigarette? Yeah, I got a cigarette.

TUTU: No, you know, smoke, marijuana.

CUSTOMER: You shoot marijuana in your veins?

CISCO: *(Holding his crotch invitingly.)* Hey, mister . . .

CUSTOMER: I'll tell your mother . . .

Nilsa tries to pick his pocket. Customer sees him and starts chasing him.

MALO: Oye, pana, ven acá un momento. Mira esto. ¿Le gustaría comprarse un reloj caro barato?

CUSTOMER: ¿Qué es, hombre? Déjame quieto.

MALO: No te vayas. Mira, qué lindo es este reloj.

CUSTOMER: Wha jew say? No pica la Inglish.

MALO: Who the hell is speaking English? Jesus Christ, I'm trying to do you a favor . . . an expensive watch . . . cheap . . . cheaper than cheap . . . in fact, it's so cheap that if I sell it to you any cheaper, you'd be stealing it from me.

CUSTOMER: I don't steal. No crook. Goo byy. Lea' me alone.

MALO: No, I ain't saying you steal it. I stole it to sell it to you at a steal. Look, forget about the word steal . . . I mean steal . . . hey, don't go . . . come 'ere . . . mira, qué belleza . . . look at it, man . . . I ain't going to bite you . . . mira, go on see . . . heavy, ah?

CUSTOMER: I don't see nothing.

MALO: Come a little bit closer. I don't want the police to see me. Look . . . see . . .

CUSTOMER: I don't have to get closer. I got 20/20 in both eyes. I see nothing. I don't see a thing. I don't want it. Good-bye.

MALO: Wait, wait, look, man, oye, mira . . . es un Bu-
          lova . . . BUUU-LUUU-VAAA for sixty do-
          larssss.
CUSTOMER: Buluva for sixty? Are jew kiddin' me? I
          could get it for forty dollars in the store.
MALO: You can get a Longine for forty dollars?
CUSTOMER: Longine, you said a Bulova.
MALO: It is a Bulova. I mean it's a Bulova watch with a
          Logine band. It's what they call a Bulogine. You
          musta heard the commercials on t.v., you do have
          a t.v.? "If it's a Bulogine, it's real keen," right?
CUSTOMER: Yes, sí, sí, I got a t.v., everybody has a t.v.
MALO: No, because if you don't have one, I can get you
          a nice t.v. . . . color . . . cheap . . . very nice
          buy.
CUSTOMER: Bulogine, huh?
MALO: Okay, dig this: I'll let you have it for sixty dol-
          lars, and when you come back for the t.v. . . . .
CUSTOMER: Sixty dollars? Thirty-five dollars is the
          most money I can afford. I don't want no t.v.
MALO: Thirty-five dollars for a Bulogine . . . what you
          take me for?
CUSTOMER: I take you for nothing, because you are
          nothing . . . a junkie . . . tecato.
MALO: Okay, it's true, I'm a dope fiend, pero no tengo
          el bicho de cartón.
CUSTOMER: Thirty-five dollars, that's it, no more, no
          less . . . maybe less . . . but no more.
MALO: Look, man, forty dollars . . . please . . . if I
          wasn't sick, you think I'd be selling this watch?
          My wife bought it for me last week. Look, when
          you come back for the t.v. I'll give it to you
          cheaper by five . . . no, ten dollars.
CUSTOMER: Wait a minute. I don't want no t.v., color
          or black and white. I don't know where you got

that idea from. If you want forty dollars, you don't want to sell the watch to me. Maybe somebody else will pay you sixty or forty dollars, but not me. Thirty-five dollars and that's it . . . take it or leave it. I got to go home. Good-bye.

MALO: Okay, okay, you got it. Thirty-five dollars. You drive a hard bargain. Listen, can you throw in a dollar for me to eat? Just a dollar? Please, I'm hungry.

CUSTOMER: Okay, here. *(Walking away.)* Qué soqueta . . . thirty-five dollars for a Bulogine.

MALO: Thirty-five dollars for a Bulogine . . . some people you can see them coming a mile away . . . a seven dollar Timex with a famous label. Hi, I'm Malo the Merchant. Malo in Spanish means bad, not bad as in bad, but bad as in good. They call me Malo the Merchant because I'm good at what I do. I'm so good, it's terrible. It's bad, that's why I'm Malo-bad. Can you dig it? What do I do? You just witnessed me in action. Some of my friends say I can talk the handle off a pot. I've never tried, but I don't doubt that I can do it. That's one of the tools of my trade: my tongue and these labels. I got all kinds of labels. The little woman at home hard at work sewing on famous labels on second-hand clothes. After I take them out the cleaners, just like new. Maybe you'll like a suit . . . very cheap . . . *(Laughs.)* . . . yeah . . . I can take a cheaply made t.v. set from some obscure company from a country you never even heard of and give glory with my labels and with my tongue . . . here, take a look at this tongue of mine . . . see it . . . all red with the fire of speech. I could have been a preacher . . . hell-fire and brimstone . . . don't think I ain't hip to the mind game . . .

turned around collar . . . shit, only thing is my words kept falling out of the bible . . . and then once I got caught in bed with the preacher's wife . . . weren't too bad . . . if he hadn't decided to join us . . . three is a crowd. Malo the Merchant . . . I like my own name . . . it's got a certain ring to it . . . everybody needs some type of recognition . . . I ain't no different than anyone else. I thought of being a dealer one time, but like you really don't make no bread. If you is a small timer, too many people to be paid, too many people come up short. Burglary is climbing too high and as you go up, so can you come down. I hate mugging. First of all, you're taking someone's payday check, 'cause not many mug the big execs. As a merchant I only take what they were goin' to waste on beers in some greasy spoon saloon. Then sometime you hit a drunk that wants to fight and you got to off him or he vomits all over you and you stink so bad ain't no pusher wanna sell you a thing. Now, I know, 'cause you see me greasy as a porkchop you think I stink. Well, this is only an accessory of my trade. I got more veins at home than a little bit . . . got it like the feds . . . everyone likes to deal and wheel. Me, I just wheel the deals. I got something for everybody. Nobody goes away empty-handed when you come and see Malo the Merchant. . . . White boys from the suburbs . . . in a way I am the cause of the state's great concern with drugs nowadays. When they came to me, I got it for them . . . never turn one of them down. They came, I gave, they took and they all got hooked, kinda like a poem. That's when dope became a terrible plague, destroying the youth of our nation. Well, not my nation, their nation, 'cause for years it had been destroying our nation and no one gave a good fuck about it. Hey, what you wanna git, whitey? Hey, whacha wanna git, Mr. Jones? You wanna nicey girlie to fuckie fuckie? I got two of everything, three of anything and you got to start out with one of nothing so you can end up with something. Someone at sometime has been taken for his poke by the sleight of hand of the Murphy Man or the words some con man spoke. Now, the dope fiends are ruining the name of a hell of a game. When are we gonna yell out no more fucking dope? You are surprised that I, a dope fiend, would make such a distinction between me and my peers? But you see, the time before this there was the time before that and that's where I live, in the time before this.

HECTOR: My father said Malo can rap and lie, I mean LIE. My father said Malo should be a politician or a newspaper man, 'cause he can lie like a book.

CHINA: *(Holding a radio.)* Hey, listen to this. *(Music gets louder. Everybody begins dancing.)*

Lucky enters and interrupts the dance.

LUCKY: Hey, bitch, where's my money?

SUGAR: What money?

LUCKY: My money, bitch, the money you're supposed to be out here hustling.

SUGAR: Get the fuck off me.

PEOPLE IN CROWD: Wooooooo! Go on girl! Do it! Tell him about himself, etc.

LUCKY: What do you think this is, Disneyland? I want my money!

SUGAR: Don't hit me. Who the fuck you think you are? Here I'm out on the street hustling to buy you

132

clothes, keep you nice and warm in the house, put the gasoline in the car so that you can drive around with some fine white girl?! Boy you better dig yourself before you be by yourself.

Lucky grabs her, twists her arms.

LUCKY: We'll talk about that upstairs, bitch.

Lucky bumps into Tutu.

TUTU: Why don't you watch where you're going, man?

Pause and silence.

LUCKY: Excuse me, bro.

Lucky sends Sugar to the apartment.

CLEARNOSE HENRY: I'm Clearnose Henry. That's what everybody calls me. Clearnose Henry . . . 'cause I always clear my nose before I blow my mind. Costs me two first presidents to buy me a box of tubes and coin Lincolns to cop my dream brown paper bag. I don't slink around corners under street lamps to score, or hide in some dim lighted muggers' tenement hall for my pusher to appear. That bag is for dope fiends and that scene is a dragpot. Grass is too scarce in these parts and I'm scared of scag 'cause I'm scared of needles . . . faint at the sight of one. That's why I don't watch those doctor shows on t.v. Excuse me a second while I pour my tubes into my dream brown paper bag. Yeah man, that looks pretty good. Like I was saying, snuff is for old people

133

who like to sit and nod and LSD or sunshine . . .
those trips they take you on are too far out . . .
speed kills . . . oh, oh, . . . the sleep sand is rain-
ing out the bottom of my dream brown paper bag.
I'm going to do it, ain't gonna talk it.

*Clearnose takes a sniff, then two, then a bunch faster and
faster. He goes into wows, ahhhs, yeahs, wows.*

*Lucky's apartment. Enter Lucky pushing Sugar into the room.
Lucky takes off his belt, strokes it and then whips Sugar.*

LUCKY: You like embarrassing me, right? ¿Te gusta?
SUGAR: But you're nothin' but a dog.

Lucky intensifies beating.

LUCKY: Who the fuck you calling a dog, bitch? Why
           weren't you making no money? *(Lucky stops beat-
           ing Sugar. He puts his belt around his neck, he
           lights a cigarette and exits.)*

*Sugar is lying on the bed. Her jones is coming down. She is in
pain, she searches around for her dope. Finding nothing, she
falls back on the bed.*

SUGAR: Mama-Mama-Mama, can you hear me, Mama?
           It's me, Mama, it's your baby, Mama.
           Papa done hit me again, Mama.
           He was drunk, Mama. I know he ain't my Papa,
               Mama,
           but every time you're sleeping he comes into the
               room,
           he comes and sits on my bed and feels on my
               leg, Mama.

Mama, he scares me when he's like that,
breathing all hard and fast and hot, spit falling
    on me,
him shaking and groaning like an animal.
I know, Mama . . . the landlord . . . the
    food . . .
Mama, where are you?
I didn't mean for you to die like you did
but you told me you'd be around
when I needed you.
Mama, where have you been?
Mama, where have you been?
Mama, where have you been?
Mama, I need you.
I love you.
I need you now, Mama. I need you now.
I needed you then.
And you tell me to wait 'til tomorrow,
tomorrow is here, Mama.
It's here and it's now yesterday, Mama.
Mama, where have you been?
Shit, Mama, I'm getting sick.
Mama, me, your baby, I needs me a fix.
Mama, I'm a junkie, Mama,
A HOPE TO DIE DOPE FIEND.
Mama, please, it beginning to hurt.
My legs, Mama, they hurt like hell.
Mama, someone is crushing them to nothing,
into powder, Mama,
into powder, Mama, white powder, Mama,
like the one I needs,
like I needed you, Mama,
like when I laid in the bed crying
from fear of the many papas
that came into my room.

Like I needed you, Mama. I needed to put my
    head between
the hollow of your breast, Mama,
like the johns need to put their heads between
    the hollow
of my breasts, Mama, and call me Mama.
Mama, they call me trickie now 'cause I've
    turned more tricks in one night
than you turn in a lifetime. *(Screams.)*
Mama, it getting worse.
The monkey is traveling down my back,
calling to my mind to feed my veins.
Mama, please help me, Mama. I'm tired of
    turning tricks,
committing crimes. I wanna kick, I wanna fix.
I want you to need me.
Mama, I can do it with your help,
with your care, your love.
Mama, love me like you mean it Mama.
The pain open the door.
Help me, Mama, please help me, please,
    please, Mama,
I-I-I . . .
SHIT, YOU IS DEAD.

Hector enters the apartment, sits a short distance from Sugar.

HECTOR: I remember her. She used to babysit me. She
used to take me to the park. She used to buy me
ice cream and candy and all that shit. She was
fine, she was nice, but now she's a shank! Now,
when she sees me, she asks me for money, 'cause
she knows I work at the A & P.

Hector leaves the apartment, a siren is heard, Lucky comes up running across the stage, knocks Hector down, yells at him, runs over to China.

LUCKY: *(To China.)* Hold this for me!
CHINA: What is it?
LUCKY: Just hold it, bitch. I'll be back later.

Tutu walks in. Hector's crying on the floor.

TUTU: *(To China.)* What happened to him?
CHINA: Some dude knocked him down.
HECTOR: Tutu, Tutu, some man hit me with a baseball bat and kicked me in the stomach and took my money.
TUTU: He took all your money?
HECTOR: Yeah, 50 cents. Oh, my leg, my leg!
TUTU: *(To China.)* Who knocked him down?
CHINA: You know the dude: Lucky the pimp. He gave me some coke and money to hold.
TUTU: Some what?
CHINA: Some coke and money to hold.
TUTU: What are you, crazy, stupid or what?
CHINA: No, man, Tutu, I just didn't have time to give it back. I didn't know what it was, anyway.
TUTU: Man, shut up. Give me that shit, and when he comes you tell him I got it.

Tutu picks up Hector.

TUTU: Come on Hector, I'll buy you an ice cream.

Tutu and Hector exit. Enters Lucky, straight to China.

LUCKY: Okay, give me my shit.
CHINA: Don't you think your shit is where it belongs: up your ass?

LUCKY: Come on, I ain't got time for your shit.
CHINA: I already told you, your shit is where it belongs, up your ass.
LUCKY: What, you crazy bitch, you trying to beat me?

Hector enters, runs by him.

HECTOR: You big bully, you maricón, you . . .

Tutu enters.

TUTU: Excuse me, brother, you got your face on my woman.
LUCKY: Your woman gots something of mine.
TUTU: *(To China.)* You got something that belongs to him?
CHINA: No.
TUTU: See, my woman got nothing of yours. Later.

Lucky grabs Tutu by the arm.

TUTU: You got hand problems or something?
LUCKY: I told you, your woman got something that belongs to me. I was running from the cops and I needed someone to dish it on, and your broad was standing there, so I dished it on her.
TUTU: You think my woman is dumb?
LUCKY: She is dumb. She took the shit.
TUTU: Man I don't want to hear that shit.

Lucky touches Tutu.

TUTU: Now, I told you before about your hands. You got a problem, man?
LUCKY: There's no problem. You got something of mine and I want it back.

138

TUTU: Well, there is a problem because, you see . . .
           (He starts laughing.)
LUCKY: What's so funny, man? Let me in on the joke.
TUTU: You're the joke, brotherman, because you see I
           got your shit and you ain't getting it back.
LUCKY: I don't want to hear that shit.
TUTU: But you're hearing it.
LUCKY: Motherfucker.
TUTU: Let me tell you, sucker, don't write a check your
           ass can't cash. *(Pushes him.)* Back up and live.
LUCKY: Wait a second, brotherman, why fight, let's
           talk. We're in the same boat. You're hustling out
           here, I'm hustling out here, you watch my back,
           I'll watch your back. There's plenty of space out
           here for both of us, plenty of money. *(He catches
           Tutu off guard, hits him in the stomach and jabs
           him in the back of the neck. He runs toward
           China, grabs her by her throat, tears at her
           clothes.)*

*The crowd yelling: "Get up, Tutu, get up. Get him, Tutu, etc."
Tutu grabs him and throws him back. He falls back, Lucky
pulls a knife.*

TUTU: What are you going to do with that, mother-
           fucker?
LUCKY: I'm goin' to cut you if you get in my way.
TUTU: You're gonna what?
LUCKY: You heard me, motherfucker. I'm gonna cut
           your black ass. Get out of my way.
TUTU: Go on, cut me, go on, punk, cut me. Mother-
           fucker, you don't even know how to use a knife.
           Go on, sucker, cut me. Go on, shoot your best.

Tutu grabs the knife from Lucky. Lucky falls to the floor. The crowd is yelling "Kill that motherfucker." China is yelling "Cut him, Tutu, get him." Tutu has Lucky on the floor.

TUTU: I ought to cut your face for pulling a knife on me.
LUCKY: Don't cut my face, don't cut my face. Take my money, but don't cut my face.

Clearnose gets too close to the fight.

TUTU: Get out of the way, Clearnose, get out of the way.

Lucky jumps and runs into the knife. Sugar screams and Malo holds her back. The action freezes.

HECTOR: *(From the top of the roof.)* Everybody wants the king of the mountain to fall. That's why I don't play that game, because when you fall, you fall hard, and you get stomped with football shoes, and that's why I don't play that game.
PANCHO: *(Grabbing Cisco by the throat.)* Where you think you going, punk. What do you think this is, a game? This ain't no play, hustling is for real. Stay here and watch him die. You may never get another chance to see a pimp fall.
CISCO: Leave me alone, leave me alone . . . *(Runs to the stoop and cries.)*
NILSA: Hey blood, you all right, you want to go to the hospital? *(She goes through his pockets at the same time, taking his shoes and his watch, etc.)*
MALO: The cop, the cop!

Light dim and Clearnose is on the roof.

CLEARNOSE: The city is drowning under tons of tubes of glue. Wow, the sky has backed away and the stars are doing the bugaloo blues. The buildings look like giant tubes of glue and the garbage cans hold mountains of jewels sparkling for my eyes to see. Man, I is a prophet. I am Jesus Christ reincarnated, one of the most outasight images I've pulled from my dream brown paper bag. Can you imagine a world without glue? You gots to have glue, you need it to hold the world together . . . and it's store bought. I better keep my imagination open for the cops. They found out I was with Frankie. He was my gluehead partner. We used to paste the world together up on the roofs, in the school toilets, in the subway trains. Oh, yeah, I was with him when he jumped into the tracks. That's the day the A-train became the B, dig it, B for blood. Wow, don't you git it? It's a heavy joke. I mean, like the dude was all over the place: head one way, arms another, leg on the platform, a very untogether person. Man, like it ain't like I pushed him into the tracks. Like I don't know what they want me for . . . you know like . . . you know what I mean, you know? Right, take me a short visit into my dream brown paper bag. Yeah, that's cool. Losing much of its power now. Oh, I wish everybody would stop saying how much they care and love.

Lights dim while Clearnose mumbles.

Tap Dancing and Bruce Lee Kicks

Tap Dancing and Bruce Lee Kicks

The People in Play:

Mario or María: *A transvestite big broad, muscular, mid-twenties. Plenty of energy . . . perpetually on the border of violent insanity.*

Julio: *A man in his mid or late forties, still in good health, but after all the pain he has endured, is looking for a rest. He has seen and experienced too much in his life to be upset about real problems, yet he takes joy in small things.*

Mike Poor: *A man in his mid thirties, self educated poet-writer coming to grips with his drug use, his life and the events that produce emotional dramas in his life.*

Mele Poor: *A woman in her late twenties, highly educated and self-assured, independent, with adolescent emotions that lead to tantrums and outbursts.*

The other people in the play will appear as shadowy figures or voices.

The Time: *Now*

The Place: *An Apartment in any of America's large inner city tenement buildings sheltering second, third and fourth generations of families who sailed onto these shores in search of the American Dream. These are the men and women that took sleeping pills hoping that they could, would and should have achieved the goal that they all set out for, but they overslept.*

The Season: *Early winter and the holiday spirit is not as joyful as it was back in Dayton, Ohio in 1903.*

MARIA: Oye, mira, cabrón . . . en English, mi amor,
you fuck. . . . Esto es un culo y yo cargo conmigo
el cuerpo de una mujer que está muy bellaca . . .

JULIO: Estás bellaco.

MARIA: Tu madre.

JULIO: La tuya que es mi comadre.

MARIA: Pues, mira, hijo de la gran yegua, a ti te gusta
como soy.

JULIO: Nunca he dicho lo contrario.

MARIA: Y tú sabe' lo que soy.

JULIO: Siempre.

MARIA: A mí se me va la sangre como a otra cualquiera
y me caliento y tú no haces ningún esfuerzo para
ponerme fría.

JULIO: Déjate de esa caca ya.

MARIA: La caca está en tu boca y te la está' comiendo.

JULIO: Mira, tragadaga . . .

MARIA: Tragadaga soy, pero cómo te gusta el culo.

JULIO: A mí me encanta.

MARIA: Por eso esta' conmigo y no con tu mujer.

JULIO: Lo sabes tú.

MARIA: Y también sé que tú eres un maricón escondido,
undercover homo.

JULIO: Mira, ten cuidado con tu lengua cabrona o te vas
a tragar los dientes.

MARIA: Atrévete.

JULIO: Sigue con tus mierditas.

MARIA: Para que te las comas.

JULIO: Dame mis fucking bolsas.

MARIA: Allí sí que te jodistes, porque me las metí.

JULIO: ¿Y cuántos han muerto en tu espalda?

MARIA: Mil doscientos, pero no lo niego ni me abo-
chorno. Me encuentro orgullosa de ser lo que soy
y no como tú, siendo lo que no soy . . . pero tú
sabe' la canción, "te conozco bacalao aunque
vengas disfrasao" . . .

JULIO: *(Picks up his guitar and sings to her.)*
Quién te ha dicho
que por falta de tus besos
voy a ser un desgraciado
por tu amor
yo sé la historia de tu vida
por eso me quedo con mis amigos
en esta prisión
tú te hicistes puta de los presos
y regalastes por cigarillo tu querer
y ahora llegó el día triste de tu vida
en frente de las celdas
en tus rodillas
mamando bicho te verás
mamando bicho
es la vida que siempre vivirás

MARIA: ¿Tú sabe' qué tú puedes hacer con esa canción? . . . róbala y mándala por correo de primera clase a la más vieja de tu casa. Oye, no sé qué yo hago con un hombre que no se le para la moronga. Tú no tienes morcilla, lo que hay es salchicha.

JULIO: Cuando yo te conocí estaba seguro que mi vida contigo iba a ser como café colao, pero you turn out to be instant coffee . . . y pullao también . . . pero ahora veo que tú no haces amor . . . tú chichas por ver la leche correr.

MARIA: Si hay un carajo, allá te encuentro.

JULIO: Sí, conmigo encima y tú abajo.

MARIA: Alguién está llámandonos.

JULIO: ¿Qué es? Me cago en diez.

MARIA: Y yo en once y doce y trece.

VOICE: Hey, lady, if you need any help or if you want me to call the cops . . . I heard him threaten you and I can hear the fight from down here.

MARIA: What?

JULIO: ¿Qué es lo que dice?

MARIA: Es el cocolo de abajo más entrometío y bochin-
choso que una mujer preñá . . . quiere llamar a la
policía por mí.

JULIO: Mira, ese cabrón hijo 'e puta . . .

MARIA: Hey, why don't you mind your own fucking
business, buster?

VOICE: I thought you . . . that you might need help,
that's all, lady.

MARIA: This is my fucking husband, you nosey bastard,
and I don't need anyone coming into our fucking
life, you sucker dickhead bubble-lip nigger.

JULIO: ¿Tanto para ese mamao?

MARIA: Go jerk off on a magazine, jerkoff.

JULIO: If we needed anything, it be a cold day in hell
before we asked you, fool.

VOICE: Boy, some people you just can't offer any help at
all, especially those no speaka the English bas-
tards.

MIKE: *(From apartment next door.)* Those no speaka the
English are having a marriage fight and they didn't
ask for your intervention.

VOICE: All I was doing was trying the good neighbor
policy.

MARIA: That you, Mike? Hey, Mister, try the good
neighbor policy on your daughter, the one that's
been trying to fuck my husband after she gets out
of school.

VOICE: What? My daughter?

MARIA: That's right, your daughter. I guess this good
neighbor shit goes a long way in your family,
'cause if you ain't trying to rap to me when your
wife is out and you know my husband isn't here,
you always got some excuse to try and come here.

MIKE: He really takes that super job to heart.

MELE: He sure does. He tries that with me too.

JULIO: I think that his son goes the same way too. Those are pretty tight jeans he always wearing and he either got a broken wrist or his rings are very heavy . .

VOICE: Look I only . . .

MARIA: Well, forget it, buster.

VOICE: I will. Cherrie, what's this about you seeing that man upstairs after school? Is that true? Where's that homo brother of yours?

MARIA: A ese, yo no lo conozco. ¿Por qué la gente siempre tiene que meterse en cosas de matrimonio?

JULIO: ¿Qué estaba diciendo Mike?

MARIA: Oh, he was getting on the super too.

JULIO: Maybe we do make a lot of racket when we fight, heh?

MARIA: Maybe we make a lot of racket when we make love.

JULIO: Yo creía que you didn't get enough undercover y todo eso.

MARIA: Bueno, la canción que me cantaste wasn't exactly greatly accepted.

JULIO: Just kidding around, that's all. You know that I love you, baby.

MARIA: "I love you, baby, and it's quite all right, I need you, baby, to walk these lonely nights. Oh, pretty baby, trust in me when I say my pretty baby, don't put me down this way." *(Singing alone, then joined in by Julio in a duet a la Frankie Valle.)*

Lights go out on them as the recorded song comes on stronger and their singing grows with the volume of the song.

Lights on. The scene has shifted to Mike and Mele's apartment.

MELE: You know what some dickhead asshole did?

MIKE: What?

MELE: Check this out . . .

MIKE: What?

MELE: Someone . . . at least one of your friends . . . put a 15 fuse plug in a 20 watt slot. Man, that is a dumb jackass, dumb.

MIKE: Heehaw!

MELE: Figures.

MIKE: Well, start kicking ass.

MELE: Don't have to . . . as soon as you can find a way to get your foot out of your mouth . . . the one you hid in there yesterday . . . you'll find a means to do it yourself. I have grown to have blind faith in your abilities to succeed in doing little feats like that.

MIKE: Yeah, I'm a great fan of Ex-President Ford.

MELE: Well, at least you can chew gum and walk at the same time, though how you accomplish that is one up on me.

MIKE: That's white California humor, right?

MELE: Oh, oh, oh, tee, tee, hee, ha, hah. *(yawns.)*

MIKE: *(A la Billy Joel singing* "It's My Life".*)* I never said I was a comedian, I never said I needed a second chance, 'cause I'm a victim of circumstance . . . don't get me wrong, I still belong . . .

MELE: Not to the human race.

MIKE: I don't?

MELE: No, more to a society of successful succulent sordid sadistical sabotage suckers . . .

MIKE: Hey, speaking of Billy Joel, did I read you the new paragraph on the story I've been working on?

MELE: No, but I get a feeling that you are going to.

MIKE: Well, if you don't wanna hear it, that's all right with me.

MELE: Good, I'm glad that you didn't take it personal.

MIKE: Anyway, this is the . . . you, you read the other thing, right?

MELE: Right . . . right . . . right . . . go ahead if you're gonna torture me. Might as well get it over with fast and as painless as possible.

MIKE: *(Reading from his notes.)* Here we go.
Billy Joel's voice declared war on the silences in the single rented room that sheltered David Dancer's factory-tired body during those hours that did not require him to breath the indecency of those alien fumes. The radio blared out Joel's song. The sound was a total contrast to the belching buses creeping outside David's window. David wished he had it inside himself to capture all the sounds that invade his privacy. They painted a picture that only a Michelangelo could create: the comedy of young kids playing, the roar of teenage souped-up cars, the exploding booms of fathers and mothers over their children's sloppiness and dirt catching magnetism, the pre-teens with radios that competed with them in size and weight, screeching out the disco poetry of the Sugar Hill Gang. Billy Carter would feel at home in Central Harlem on a Sunday afternoon. David's needle-scarred arm rested on the window sill. The late spring air stirred in his hair. His eyes at half-mast, his train of thought occasionally interrupted by the chemical agents he had smuggled into his biolgical system via a hypodermic that carried the illegal substance. He smiled at his own thoughts, knowing he could never hold a nightwatchman's job.

Staying alert in his own home was a chore in itself. *(A knock on the door interrupts the reading.)* See who it is. If it's you-know-who, I ain't here.

MELE: Who . . . yeah, wait a second. Mike, where you put the new sets?

MIKE: Here.

MELE: Two for five dollars . . . see you later . . . here, all he had was four seventy-five . . . gave him a play on a quarter's.

MIKE: It comes out of your profit.

MELE: That's all right, it all goes into the same pot. Keep on with the reading. I must say, it is a little interesting.

MIKE: Naw, I'll run the rest to you later. The bastard broke off my concentration.

MELE: Well, you're the one who wanted to invest in that box of works.

MIKE: Yeah, but it is a dollar and a good one at that.

MELE: I know, but there are side effects with it, you know. Like people knowing that we are selling works and they be knocking at the door at all odd hours of the day, even when we're taking care of personal biolgocal affairs.

MIKE: Yeah . . . 30 dollars for a hundred of them sets, at three dollars a set, we make more than a 100 percent profit. So for that, I guess we have to put up with a little inconveniences now and then . . . anyway, it's better than running a shooting gallery.

MELE: Telling me . . . shit, I'd never venture into a deal like that again, like we did last year in Harlem . . . that was total shit.

MIKE: We did make good money on it though, didn't we?

MELE: Yeah, but remember all the shit that went along with it?

MIKE: How the hell can I forget? When I rented that

space ⌐n 112th street, I didn't think it would almost cause my demise.

MELE: Are you going to write that into the David Dancer Story?

MIKE: I don't know . . . never gave it that much of a thought.

MELE: Maybe you should give it a thought. I mean it, no joke. Here, use my tape recorder. Tape it down, then transfer it over and find a way to incorporate it in what you already have. *(He turns it on and her voice comes on.)*

MIKE: What's that?

MELE: Oh, something I been working on.

MIKE: You never told me you were working on a song.

MELE: Aw, well, it's not finished yet.

MIKE: Play it. Let me hear it.

MELE: When it's finished, I'll do it for you.

MIKE: Aww, come on, do it now, just what you have.

MELE: Naw, really, naw.

MIKE: Awww, you want to be petted into it. All right, please. I'm your biggest fan and I need to hear your latest song. If you don't, oh, I'll just die. Oh, please, pretty, pretty please with sugar on top . . . and honey on the side.

MELE: All right, you twisted my arm.

MIKE: Twisted your head's more like it.

MELE: It's a thing on Coltrane.
Coltrane blows
a song for the poets to dream
a cocaine dream
is the song that Coltrane brings
to me
Coltrane brings a dream with every
note
a dream of reality

drifting into illusions with every snort
blues were issued to create
Coltrane was born to create
cocaine was used to deteriorate
Coltrane blows cocaine dreams for me

MIKE: That's pretty nice and it ain't finished yet, huh? I know what. We can send your song in as a poem and get it published with my story and that'll get us some extra cash, 'cause I got a deadline on the David Dancer thing and that's gonna pay the bills and the rent. Did Richie say he was coming over today?

MELE: No, tomorrow. He left you a note when you were sleeping. He didn't want to wake you up. He said to tell you that he'll only be able to bring in a quarter of a pound instead of the half he promised. Here is the note he left you.

MIKE: Hmmm, well, it beats a blank and it's up front on consignment.

MELE: Hey, like you said, it beats a blank and you don't have to run no bread up front.

MIKE: That's why I invested in them works, you know. It's like having ready money. If you got smoke, you got money rolled up. A few shoot to forty-two and your pockets will no longer cry the blues.

MELE: You hear that shit on the T.V.?

MIKE: What was that?

MELE: Well, after the crime and the political slime had been reported, the six o'clock news ended with a cute remark about being National Secretary's week.

MIKE: Get her off your lap and take her to lunch in between her coffee breaks, if you can get her out of the restroom.

MELE: Yeah, then you heard it?

154

MIKE: No, I didn't.

MELE: You did so.

MIKE: No, really I didn't.

MELE: Then, how you know what they said?

MIKE: They really said that?

MELE: Yeah, you know it, you heard it.

MIKE: I didn't. It's just that's what I said kidding around just to think of something stupid to say.

MELE: Well, that's what they said . . . and they didn't think it was stupid. They acted like they said something intelligent. Assholes.

MIKE: The right-to-know first ammendment . . . like Mr. Friendly said, protect it from those who would destroy it and from those who love it too much . . . *(Searching through a box of clothes.)* These chothes that we bought on Orchard Street are full of birth defects.

MELE: What's wrong with them?

MIKE: Well, let me see. Here we have a pair of paraplegic pants, a mongoloide sweater . . . siamese socks . . . armless shirts . . . club foot sneakers . . .

MELE: A de luxe demented malnutrition mind vomiting humorless antagonizing anecdotes by an anthropoid with anthropomorphic qualities.

MIKE: Who the hell you studied with, Spiro Agnew?

MELE: I wish there was an antibiotic I could transmit into this inebriated android that would serve as an antidote to your ill usage of the English language to describe your pell mell state of existence.

MIKE: It had to be Spiro Agnew.

MELE: But since God has chosen for your quest to be that of a penguin, a bird that can't fly . . . and it's obvious that any penicillin will be penalized and impounded within the penitentiary . . . the penin-

sula . . . the puny peninsula that boasts your pen-
ury brain . . . so any illusion that I may have
about your penance is truly a romantic passion I
possess for the peon named Mike Poor.

MIKE: Jesus H. Christ.
MELE: In other words, you're a big mouth with bad taste
          and bad breath.

Lights out.

*When the lights are brought up the scene has shifted to an
apartment that has been turned into a shooting gallery. There
are signs on the wall indicating that such a business exists
there:*

"2.00 dollars—dos pesos"
"1.50 if you have your own work."
"Clean your works—limpien sus aparatos"
"Brand new gymics set 3.00"
"Keep the place clean"
"5.00 to hit in the neck"
"1.00 for a hit."
"Don't give money to anyone else—houseman collects
all bread"
"Cigarettes .10 cents"
"No horse playing around—no loud talking"
"When you finish please leave—no hanging out"

FLACO: Hey, man, those signs really necessary?
SOCIO: Sí, bro, they are very, really necessary.
FLACO: They are, huh?
SOCIO: Yeah, man, just like the reason I carry the shit
          paper with me. How is it? Who you cop from?
FLACO: It's half ass. I mean I feel it, but it's nothing that
          I would write home about, know what I mean? It's

156

from the Blue Club. They had something nice, but you know how that game goes.

SOCIO: The blue club? They had something half ass? Like they had a thing that was smoking . . . knock you on your fucking ass. Man, but then, bam, milk sugar . . . pero ¿qué vas a hacer? You know, man, you go out, tell these assholes that they have something worth ten dollars and the next thing you know is that they get big fucking ideas . . . more money and, wip wop wop, it's shit, it's out of range.

FLACO: Man, like I've been on the fucking program a month and clean. Then I get detoxed and zip, I'm out here again chasing the dirty low down, doggin' it again, know what I mean?

SOCIO: Me lo dice o te lo cuento, mi hermano, man? Mira, bro . . . I used to run Pepe Veneno's spots here on the avenue. You know, that used to be a smoker, right? Well, man, we ran this thing like a marine corps platoon, tú sabe' . . . hup one two three, put your hands in your pockets, pull out the green . . .

FLACO: ¡Vaya! ¿Tiene' alcohol, bro?

SOCIO: No . . . that waters clean, man . . . let's conserve, tú sabe' . . .

FLACO: So, what happen man?

SOCIO: Oh sí, yeah, like you know, man, the shit what we had was dynamite, but none of the workers would tell him that. I mean, we test it for him . . . then get some one off the streets, and they do it too. Man, that's where we blew, or better to say, that's where the dope fiends blew . . . they started telling him how good the shit was and the next thing you know, the mother starts Bruce Lee-ing the shit to death . . . put more cuts on it than Frankenstein!

157

SOCIO: Hear that?

FLACO: What?

SOCIO: That tap tap tapping shit.

FLACO: Yeah, what's that?

SOCIO: That's that dude downstairs. Day in night out the chump stay on that fucking typewriter . . . banging away. I think he's writing a book or something. I rapped with him once. Guy's from L.A.

FLACO: Is it electric? I know a dude looking for one.

SOCIO: Yeah, I think so, but, man, let me tell you something . . . I once did a job in this guy's place, right, and I stole his T.V., radio, tape recorder, everything but the kitchen sink, and I got away with the shit . . . but a week later I was in jail. The chump-ass nigger tracked me down because I took his typewriter. I mean, he didn't care about the other stuff, but the dude was a writer and that was his bread and butter, man. Since then I cool it. I mean, I won't rip off anything religious or mess around with some artist things, man. Them dudes are wierd. Most of them are out to lunch, you know what I mean?

FLACO: Yeah, them type of people who tell their wives, hey, man, I'm going out for a pack of cigarettes and you don't hear from the suckers for twenty years.

SOCIO: You finished, man?

FLACO: Yeah, man, here.

SOCIO: No, man, you clean them.

FLACO: So, you don't think it's cool to try and make the place downstairs?

SOCIO: For me, no. For you, hey, it's your world.

FLACO: Yeah, but we kinda live in the same space, you know, and if you won't eat the fruit, man, I sure ain't . . .

Knock on door.

SOCIO: Customers . . . see you later, man.
FLACO: Yeah, be back about midnight.
SOCIO: But this time leave the cotton wet.
FLACO: And two dollars too . . . yeah, well, if there's enough.
SOCIO: There'll be enough.

Lights. Return to Mike and Mele's apartment when lights come up again.

MIKE: Just about finished with this piece for Pat . . . he keeps calling from L.A.
MELE: Man must want the thing 'cause it costs money to use the phone, baby.
MIKE: You know what I would like . . . to get into every apartment here and be like a fly on the wall and be able to do a story about everything that jumps in this building . . . I mean the whole trip.
MELE: Another get rich quick scheme, man? They all turn out bust to you.
MIKE: That's *for* you, not *to* you.
MELE: *To you, for you,* who the hell cares . . . they all stink. Look, why don't you face facts?
MIKE: Like, what facts are you talking about?
MELE: Like the fact that you put our money into this bullshit drug paraphernalia and it could get us busted and there goes your career down the drain?
MIKE: If I get busted, I'm sure Pat would find a way to make it sensational.
MELE: Well, one thing, he ain't gonna do anything unless you send him that damn piece.
MIKE: Yeah . . . you wanna go back to L.A., right?
MELE: Yeah, baby, I do, but look, the Bible said "where thou goes I too shall go and your people shall be

my people and your God shall be my God."

MIKE: Cut it out . . . maybe we'll sell it all to the dude upstairs. He runs that gallery. You know, I kinda miss L.A., even if the city is three hours behind the times.

MELE: Bullshit.

MIKE: What am I going to write about?

MELE: Why ask me? I'm not the writer, you are.

MIKE: Yeah, I am, ain't I?

Phone rings.

MIKE: Hello. Hey, Pat, how's things? Yeah, I'm thinking of writing a story about the building where I live, but I can't seem to touch on anything. But I got a good idea, see, if we can do it so that we can peek into the lives of the people here . . . oh, that's been done before? Well, I . . . ah, listen, if you can send me and Mele some bread so that we can go out back to the coast . . . no, by bus.

MELE: Bus? You crazy?

MIKE: Shhh . . . yeah, I'll write about traveling out to the coast . . . the people, of course. I can't seem to get a grip on things here. Yeah, man, Western Union.

MELE: Bus? Are you crazy?

Mike keeps typing with Mele ranting at him. Lights.